WITH MODERN MEDICINE has come longer life spans and, thus, more years to spend in service to the Kingdom. Culture, however, would encourage us to take it easy during the twilight years because "we've earned it." John Goodale offers a convicting and inspiring reminder that the Lord is not done with us until the moment He calls us home.

—**Jim Daly**, President, *Focus on the Family*

FOR THE LAST FIVE DAYS I have luxuriated in reading every word of this book by John Goodale. He has brought to its writing the same gracious, earnest integrity that I have observed for the past three plus decades in his personal life as well as substantial pastoral ministry. With great insight he has addressed the major topics of contemporary living—viewing them all through the lens of earthy biblical characters, encouraging relevant literature and his own life experience. And he has done it in a way that is most informative, inspirational and challenging. As one just now turning 80 years old, I have found it a most helpful guide to my own deep desire to finish well!

—**John Huffman**, Pastor Emeritus, St. Andrew's Presbyterian Church, Newport Beach, CA and former board chair of World Vision, *Christianity Today* and Gordon-Conwell Theological Seminary

---

JOHN'S PERSONAL DESIRE TO FINISH WELL rewards his readers with warm insights on life and faith. This is a pastor who loves and values others deeply, and a man who wants his life remembered for the love that comes from Jesus. Your own next chapter will be enriched by spending time in these chapters full of insights to help us finish well."

—**Tim McConnell**, lead pastor at First Pres Colorado Springs and author of *Happy Church*

JOHN GOODALE HAS WRITTEN A BOOK THAT'S A GIFT to everyone in the last third of their lives. Distilling decades of pastoral experience and drawing on a deep well of biblical resources, Goodale helps his readers chart satisfying, purpose-filled pathways for the rest of their lives. His reflective questions ensure that the book is not just a good read, but also an effective one. While the book is targeted for those nearing or in retirement, *Finishing Well* should also be required reading for young adults who are *starting hopefully*. It will provide great wisdom as they look to the future. We all want to hear the words, "Well done, good and faithful servant."

—**Eunice McGarrahan**, Retired Associate Pastor, The National Presbyterian Church, Washington, D.C.

FINISHING WELL

Biblical Lessons
to Maximize Your Later Years

FINISHING WELL

Biblical Lessons
to Maximize Your Later Years

John Goodale

East of the Mountains and West of the Sun

RHYOLITE PRESS LLC
Colorado Springs, Colorado

Published in the United States of America

RHYOLITE PRESS LLC
P.O. Box 60144
Colorado Springs, Colorado 80960
www.rhyolitepress.com

Goodale, John
FINISHING WELL
Biblical Lessons to Maximize Your Later Years
All scripture references use the NIV translation unless otherwise noted

1st printing: August, 2020

Library of Congress Control Number: 2020915186

ISBN 978-1-943829-15-6

Publisher's Cataloging-in-Publication Data

Names: Goodale, John, author.

Title: Finishing well : Biblical lessons to maximize your later years / John Goodale.

Description: Colorado Springs, CO: Rhyolite Press, 2020.

Identifiers: LCCN: 2020915186 | ISBN: 978-1-943829-15-6

Subjects: LCSH Aging--Biblical teaching. | Older people in the Bible. | Middle-aged persons--Religious life. | Spiritual formation. | Older Christians--Religious life. | Aging--Religious aspects--Christianity. | BISAC RELIGION / Biblical Reference / Quotations | RELIGION / Biblical Reference / Quotations | SELF-HELP / Spiritual | FAMILY & RELATIONSHIPS / Life Stages / Later Years

Classification: LCC BV4579.5 G66 2020 | DDC 248.8/4--dc23

PRINTED IN THE UNITED STATES OF AMERICA
Book layout and cover design: Donald Kallaus
Front cover photograph: Perica Oreskovic—Unsplash

To my bride and life partner, Deborah, who makes me better. And to our First Pres faithful, who have encouraged my growth for 25 years.

CONTENTS

INTRODUCTION

"Most people spend less time planning the last season of their life than they do organizing their next two-week vacation."
—James Houston and Michael Parker

I learned a valuable lesson one summer at the age of 17. I was a member of our high school cross-country team, and competed in an eight-mile Saturday race at a nearby town. Though this race occurred more than 40 years ago, I still remember three things about it. People gathered at the start of the race to cheer us on, and I remember their applause and my adrenalin propelling me near the front of the pack. I also remember running out of steam a mile or two later, because my early pace wasn't sustainable. My most vivid memory is of laboring so slowly along the remaining miles, I finished ahead of only two other participants in their 70s—*very* embarrassing for a teenager.

My lesson that day? Important as good beginnings are, it's the quality of finish that ultimately defines a race. By the same token, we're generally remembered among family and friends more for how we live out our later years than for what we accomplished during initial decades.

How we begin does have a tremendous impact upon both races and life. A sprinter's finishing time is aided by a fast start. Similarly, a home environment during formative years (affirming or critical words, habits taught or neglected, love given or withheld) can greatly influence our launch into adulthood. Good starts often reap dividends.

But it's also true that a poor finish can offset a good beginning. Well-intentioned New Year's resolutions are annually abandoned within weeks due to poor follow-through on longed-for changes. Relentless distractions can also tug us away from good beginnings on important priorities. We may start things easily and with great enthusiasm, but it matters little in the long run if we don't finish well—as I witnessed during another running experience.

I grew up in Washougal, Washington (try saying that quickly five times), which annually sponsored a March of Dimes Walk-athon. Participants raised donations to fund birth defect research for the miles they walked; additionally, the first person finishing the 20-mile course received a savings bond (remember those?). During my senior year of high school, I earned that prize by running the course. As others began walking that day, I started jogging. For some reason, a young boy decided to run with me. Though he stayed with me the first half-mile or so, I remember sadly thinking that he couldn't sustain the pace—and that his walk for the day would end badly as a result. Sure enough, he eventually slowed to a very labored walk.

Poet Henry Wadsworth Longfellow noted, "**Great is the art of the beginning, but greater is the art of ending.**" Israel's earliest kings certainly provide sad examples of this. Solomon was given greater wisdom at a young age than anyone else possessed; however, "As Solomon grew old, his wives turned his heart after other gods, and his heart was not fully devoted to the Lord his God" (I Kings 11:4). Following Solomon's disappointing finish, God gave Jeroboam rule over 10 of Israel's 12 tribes—but later declared to him, "You have done more evil than all who lived before you" (I Kings 14:9).

Then there's David. What a great start: described as a man after God's heart, anointed Israel's king by the prophet Samuel, and victorious over the giant warrior Goliath. But this good beginning was overshadowed by disappointing later years. David committed adultery with Bathsheba, then murdered her husband to hide his actions. David's parenting also fell short: he failed to act decisively when a son (Amnon) raped one of his daughters (Tamar), then didn't discipline another son (Absalom) who killed Amnon to avenge his sister. Not only was David surprised by Absalom's later attempt to overthrow him, he was oblivious to another son's plot (Adonijah) to take the throne near the end of David's life. David also brought disaster upon his people late in life by overruling the advice of others and counting the size of his army. David's life was admirable in many ways, but his finish left much to be desired.

With the average life expectancy in America increasing during the past century from roughly 50 years of age to around 80, we now have an opportunity to meaningfully live out additional decades that were unavailable to our grandparents. This book is an invitation to make the most of the years still before you. *Desire* to finish well is good—but desire, coupled with *intentionality*, is even better.

In the pages ahead, we'll explore stories of men and women in the Bible. Yes, it can be difficult to connect with customs and circumstances that are centuries removed from and dramatically different from our reality today. But these long-ago stories also contain elements of life still applicable to our stories today. Reflecting upon the connective nature of stories, James Smith wrote, "We were made not just to enjoy stories but to enter them. We long to take our lives, our stories, and merge them with another story." We'll do just that as we consider these qualities of finishing well:

- Living with purpose (Joshua);
- Seizing daily opportunities (Esther);
- Leaving a legacy (Abraham);
- Maintaining meaningful relationships (Moses);
- Understanding our potential (Gideon);
- Feeling valued (Zacchaeus);
- Expressing gratitude (A woman who anointed Jesus);
- Experiencing peace (Mary, the mother of Jesus);
- Trusting God's timing (Jairus);
- Finding strength (David);
- Seeing a big picture (Elijah);
- Maintaining overflowing cups (Mary and Martha);
- Cultivating hope (Habakkuk); and
- Developing courage (Joshua, part 2).

Four larger chapter groupings provide different angles for viewing our lives. Our first set of stories prompts an *outward* examination of what we still have to offer this world. We'll then take an *inward* look at qualities that impact our approach to life. Our third direction looks *upward* as we seek to confidently follow God's leading into an unknown and sometimes challenging future. Finally, we'll look *forward* by considering qualities that can propel us into the years ahead. All scripture references use the NIV translation unless otherwise noted.

One more thing. Throughout each chapter, you'll find questions to help you think personally about what you're reading. As you encounter each one, I encourage you to pause and ponder your response before turning the page. Allow these to become sacred moments between you and your Creator that lead you into deeper insights about yourself.

I was also on the track team during high school, and one of my races was the mile. It consisted of four laps around the track; rather than waiting for a final sprint at the end of the race, I always tried to quicken my pace when the final lap began. After thirty years of ministry, I hope for another eight to ten in my current ministry setting, God and church willing. Thinking of my mile race, this means I'm now on my final ministry lap. Additionally, I just turned 60, which means that another third of my years could still lie ahead. My desire to finish well in both life and ministry has been a catalyst for articulating and living out many of this book's lessons. I want to maintain a strong pace well before the finish line approaches.

As our church's Pastor of Caring Ministries, I've been blessed to work with many members who are doing their best to finish well. Watching and listening to them over the years has influenced my understanding of what it means to move well toward the finish line of our lives, however far or near it may be for each of us. I hope I've also been an encouragement to these dear saints along the way—just as I hope the following words will equip and encourage you to finish well.

I'm grateful for the lesson about finishing well that a painful race taught me many years ago. After learning from my experience, I returned to the same race the next summer, skipped the rushed start, finished with a great time—and had a lot more fun. We all continue learning new things throughout life, no matter how small the lessons or how far along we are on our journey. I pray that these stories and observations will prompt new thinking and intentionality that help you finish well this race of life you're running. May you one day declare as triumphantly as the Apostle Paul, "I have finished the race" (II Timothy 4:7).

PART I
LOOKING AROUND

Chapter 1

YOU'RE NOT DONE YET

"One of the saddest experiences is to awaken at old age and discover that one has been using only a small part of self."
—Gordon McDonald

I once read of an elderly man with Alzheimer's who lived with his son. One day the man borrowed his son's truck to run errands in a nearby town. But after backing out of the driveway, he became disoriented. He was driving but suddenly unsure of his destination. He was passing through town but didn't know why. When his road merged onto a freeway, the man simply continued driving. The state police eventually found him sitting quietly in the truck on the freeway shoulder 60 miles away, out of gas and unsure how he'd gotten there.

This story offers a sad reminder of Alzheimer's devastating effects upon many. It also illustrates our potential to move through life on auto-pilot, even without this disease. Perhaps daily responsibilities or activities regularly propel us forward, without a larger purpose to remind us where we're heading or why. Long-term goals may seem less important later in life than during earlier years. Well-developed routines make it easier to coast. **Cruise control feels pretty good—until we eventually find ourselves wondering where we're headed or how we ended up where we are.**

I discovered the value of looking out ahead as a teenager when learning to drive. The first time I got behind the wheel, I instinctively fixed my attention on the front hood of the car; that seemed the best way to keep this large vehicle moving in the right direction. I was quickly taught to gaze at the road further out ahead and discovered that my steering became more effective when I did.

Finishing well requires a similar long-range gaze that keeps us moving forward in meaningful ways. This larger direction prevents us from slipping into a pattern of simply allowing daily routine to direct us. Purpose influences daily choices and activity. As naturalist Henry David Thoreau explained his simple living in nature for two years, "I went to the woods because I wished to live deliberately . . . and not, when I came to die, discover that I had not lived."

After speaking on this subject to a group of retired church members a few years ago, I was delighted to receive this email response from one of them: "At 80 I was thinking perhaps I was nearing time to speak to you about my eventual passing. I just discovered I have a lot of living still to do." Our first story of Joshua illustrates the importance of purposefully looking forward, whatever our age. It also reminds us that we can easily drift without realizing it.

Joshua's Story

Joshua was one of 12 spies Moses sent to explore the Promised Land before the Israelites entered; upon their return, only he and Caleb reported that the land could be conquered with God's help. Unfortunately, the Israelites listened to the other 10 spies who expressed fear about the land's challenges. The nation's lack of faith prevented them from setting foot in the land for another 40 years; when they did, Joshua and Caleb were the only ones from that generation allowed to enter. Joshua served as Moses' assistant during their years of waiting and became the nation's leader after Moses died. He then led the Israelites in conquering the Promised Land during the latter half of the thirteenth century B.C. Joshua's accomplishments over the years were substantial—but God's initial greeting suggests that he might have started coasting a bit:

> When Joshua had grown old, the LORD said to him, "You are now very old, and there are still very large areas of land to be taken over. This is the land that remains: all the regions of the Philistines and Geshurites, from the Shihor River on the east of Egypt to the territory of Ekron on the north, all of it counted as Canaanite though held by the five Philistine rulers in Gaza, Ashdod, Ashkelon, Gath and Ekron; the territory of the Avvites on the south; all the land of the Canaanites, from Arah of the Sidonians as far as Aphek and the border of the Amorites; the area of Byblos; and all Lebanon to the east, from Baal Gad below Mount Hermon to Lebo Hamath.
>
> "As for all the inhabitants of the mountain regions from Lebanon to Misrephoth Maim, that is, all the Sidonians, I myself will drive them out before the Israelites. Be sure to allocate this land to Israel for an inheritance, as I have instructed you, and divide it as an inheritance among the nine tribes and half of the tribe of Manasseh." (Joshua 13:1-7)

It's one thing to joke about our increasing years—such as these indications that we're growing older:

- *Your address book has mostly names that start with Doctor;*
- *It takes longer to rest than it did to get tired;*
- *Your idea of a night out is sitting on the patio; or*
- *You sink your teeth into a steak—and they stay there.*

It can be annoying when someone else comments about our age. But it's *really* something if God tells us we're old, as He did Joshua.

After the Lord's initial acknowledgement of Joshua's age, we'd expect words of praise for all that he'd accomplished. Following Moses' leadership surely wasn't easy, nor was transitioning his people from desert nomads to a conquering nation, then to settled inhabitants. Joshua faithfully provided leadership the Israelites needed as they made this new land their own. But instead of encouraging him to kick back and let someone else do the heavy lifting, the Lord nudged Joshua with more to do. Pockets of resistance needed to be cleaned out and the land divided among the tribes.

If it was necessary for God to remind Joshua what still had to be done, could that mean Joshua had lost sight of these things? Had Joshua started looking at accomplishments behind him more than looking ahead to what he could still do? While we don't know the dynamics behind this interaction, God's instruction suggests that Joshua may have needed reminding of opportunities still ahead. So, the Lord provided it. Joshua accomplished far more than most ever will—but despite this and the fact that he was very old, God knew he still had more to offer. The Lord wasn't finished accomplishing His purposes through Joshua.

If we read further, we'd discover that Joshua got the message; the remainder of this book describes his faithful response to God's nudge to continue pouring out his life. That's God's desire for us as well—that we not settle for what we've accomplished but continue looking forward to use our lives as fully as possible. As Bob Buford put it, "(God) has created a grand narrative for you to live out and is determined to prevent you from writing a smaller, less significant part than the one he has already written." It's not that our Lord is a hard taskmaster—He just longs for each of us to make the most of the life He's given us.

Pastor Craig Groeschel declared, "**If you're not dead, you're not done!**" Let's consider what this means for us.

Our Story

Joshua's story offers a helpful caution against pulling back in life sooner than we should. Former Supreme Court Justice Oliver Wendell Holmes noted this inclination to utilize less of our lives, stating, "Many die with their music still in them." God has placed within each of us a unique song of gifting, experience and passion— our music to sing until our final day in this world. Finishing well requires a resistance to settling for music that's already emerged from our lives, and a refusal to believe our best performance is in the past. Our lives can be like music compositions that beautifully conclude by building upon earlier patterns in the piece. Regardless of our age or what we've already accomplished, God longs to draw more new music from our lives.

What words best describe your life's music thus far? How do you feel about that description?

The Dash by Linda Ellis describes the mark separating our years of birth and death. Her poem encourages us to make the most of what occurs between these bookends of life; though we can't control these dates, we *can* influence what fills our dash. And later years are as important to the substance of our dash as earlier ones. Benjamin Franklin was 78 years old when he created bifocals. Thomas Edison submitted his final patent at the age of 83. Michelangelo was still working on the dome of St. Peter's Basilica in Rome in his 80s. In 2017, nine of the ten people who won Nobel prizes for science or economics were over 70 years old. Though our remaining accomplishments may pale compared to these, let's remain open to—even expectant of—what God still has in store for us. Former President Jimmy Carter offered this encouragement:

> "If we have not achieved our early dreams, we must either find new ones or see what we can salvage from the old. If we have accomplished what we set out to do in our youth, then we need not weep like Alexander the Great that we have no more worlds to conquer. There is clearly much left to be done, and whatever else we are going to do, we had better get on with it."

Living into the new territory of experiences God still has for us can sometimes feel challenging, even overwhelming. That's because current activity is often shaped by familiar and comfortable patterns. We return to the same restaurant because we've previously enjoyed meals there. We take the same route home when driving around town. Returning to vacation destinations we know may feel more comfortable than navigating new experiences in unfamiliar locations. Returning to the familiarity of prior experiences often makes life easier. But much about our current and future seasons of life will always remain new. Though we learned valuable lessons while navigating our 60's, our 70's introduce new challenges, as will subsequent decades. We're regularly encountering new experiences during our later years—and we're doing our best to navigate them well.

Joshua was told by God, "there are still very large areas of land to be taken over." Much land also remains before each of us—new land of experiences, lessons, and contributions. As Walter Wright put it in *The Third Third of Life*, "Pray to be spent. Give all you can. Don't die with anything in the reserves." Let's explore three ways we can seek to do this during the years still ahead.

1. Correct Any Drift

Swedish chemist Alfred Nobel made a fortune inventing powerful explosives and selling the formula to governments that weaponized them. When his brother died, a newspaper accidentally printed Alfred's obituary, identifying him as the inventor of dynamite who made a fortune helping armies achieve new levels of mass destruction. Nobel was dismayed to discover a legacy that he didn't desire. He subsequently altered his dash by establishing an endowment for the Nobel Prizes, which award achievements in the arts and sciences.

Nobel's mistaken obituary prompted a desire to make his life count for more. Even if we lack a similar dramatic moment, we can periodically pause to examine whether we're moving in the direction we desire. Such times of reflection create opportunities to correct discrepancies between where we'd like to be and where we are. The longer it takes to notice any places of drift, the more effort it may take to get back on track.

Whenever one of my high school cross-country races was held in an out of the way location, there was potential to get off course if the path wasn't marked well or runners weren't paying attention. Fortunately, I don't remember a time when this happened to me— but it can occur all too frequently in life. Peoples' final years usually don't end poorly because individuals suddenly or spectacularly veered off course. More often, they weren't paying attention to a gradual erosion of values, priorities, and direction.

My dad died 10 years ago of pancreatic cancer. If there was any good to this horribly aggressive disease, it's that he had two years to get his house in order; he was able to say and hear important messages that needed to be communicated. None of us can count on similar advance warnings that our finish line is near. But we can proactively identify and correct areas of drift today that will help ensure a good finish tomorrow.

What habits or choices may be creating gradual drift from where you want to be?

2. Identify Purpose

When three stonecutters were asked what they were doing, the first replied that he was simply cutting stones. The second stonecutter responded that he was making a living to support his family. The third stonecutter, however, proudly answered that he was building a cathedral. Understanding great purpose added meaning to the third stonecutter's activity that the others lacked. The importance of this element prompted pastor Rick Warren to assert, "**The greatest tragedy is not death, but life without purpose.**"

Walter Wright notes, "Purpose is what gets us up in the morning, what energizes our day. Purpose motivates and channels our choices. It creates goals, objectives, strategies or hopes that pull us forward." Despite these benefits, many limit their focus to immediate priorities just out ahead. Though their days are filled with activity, they can too easily lack meaning and direction. American historian James Truslow Adams stated, "It would be a good idea, as fantastic as it sounds, to muffle every telephone, halt every motor, stop all activity one day to give people a chance to ponder for a few minutes what it's all about—why they are living and what they really want."

Fortunately, our Creator provides purpose to our days—and like Joshua, He longs for us to make the most of them. Living out the music that He's placed within us becomes easier when we ask the Lord's help to better understand the meaningful purpose to our remaining years. After all, Jesus' promise of abundant life in John 10:10 doesn't have an asterisk that nullifies this offer at a certain age. It applies as fully to years still before us as it did those behind us. Identifying purpose helps us live abundantly and to experience Roman philosopher Seneca's encouragement: "Old age is full of enjoyment if you know how to use it."

If asked to describe your present purpose—what you're steering your remaining years toward—how would you answer?

3. Keep Your Edge Sharp

When our children Matthew and Suzanne were younger, I faithfully recorded their physical growth with lines and dates on their bedroom walls. A child's growth is easy to identify and eagerly anticipated. But personal growth becomes more difficult to quantify as adults; for that reason, we pay less attention to it than we did when younger. We tend to assume that accumulated learning over the years provides all that we need to know for the years ahead. The downside is that resting upon rather than adding to what we know can dull our approach to life. Author Johann Goethe undoubtedly had this in mind when he wrote, **"We must always change, renew, rejuvenate ourselves; otherwise we harden."**

No matter how much we've learned over the years, God still has more to teach us about ourselves, Him, and how to live well. The Greek word for "disciple" comes from the verb *manthano*, meaning "to learn." If personal growth isn't currently a priority, consider what activities can keep your internal edge sharp. For example, I enjoy teaching a Sunday morning class at church because I'm pushed by the study and preparation. Others keep their minds sharp with puzzles or games, by learning a new language, or through other creative options. Henry Ford declared, "Anyone who keeps learning stays young."

Jigoro Kano understood the value of continuing to grow. The

founder of judo, Kano was at one time the highest-ranking black belt. When Kano's death approached, he reportedly asked his students to bury him wearing a white belt, the symbol of a beginner or learner. Pablo Casals, one of the world's greatest cellists, also remained a learner during his later years. Asked why he continued to practice at the age of 90, Casals responded: "Because I think I'm making progress!"

What activities currently help keep your edge sharp?

Final Thought

Remember Caleb, who with Joshua provided a minority report among Moses' 12 spies? While Joshua's leadership role increased over the years, nothing more is recorded about Caleb until the chapter immediately following Joshua's nudge from the Lord. Forty-five years after visiting the Promised Land, Caleb reappeared with a request:

> Now the people of Judah approached Joshua at Gilgal, and Caleb son of Jephunneh the Kenizzite said to him, "You know what the LORD said to Moses the man of God at Kadesh Barnea about you and me. I was forty years old when Moses the servant of the LORD sent me from Kadesh Barnea to explore the land. And I brought him back a report according to my convictions, but my fellow Israelites who went up with me made the hearts of the people melt in fear. I, however, followed the LORD my God wholeheartedly. So on that day Moses swore to me, 'The land on which your feet have walked will be your inheritance and that of your children forever, because you have followed the LORD my God wholeheartedly.'

"Now then, just as the LORD promised, he has kept me alive for forty-five years since the time he said this to Moses, while Israel moved about in the wilderness. So here I am today, eighty-five years old! I am still as strong today as the day Moses sent me out; I'm just as vigorous to go out to battle now as I was then. Now give me this hill country that the Lord promised me that day. You yourself heard then that the Anakites were there and their cities were large and fortified, but, the LORD helping me, I will drive them out just as he said."

Then Joshua blessed Caleb son of Jephunneh and gave him Hebron as his inheritance. So Hebron has belonged to Caleb son of Jephunneh the Kenizzite ever since, because he followed the LORD, the God of Israel, wholeheartedly. (Joshua 14:6-14)

Caleb demanded the hill country previously visited by the spies. This area was inhabited by the Anakites, legendary for their height and fighting ability; perhaps these were the "giants" who struck fear into the hearts of the other 10 spies. Given Caleb's description of large fortified cities, he faced a formidable foe. But Caleb wasn't intimidated. It's as if he'd spent the past 45 years dreaming of this moment, confident in what he could accomplish with God's help even at the age of 85.

Did you notice a repeated description of Caleb? The word "wholeheartedly" occurs three times (Joshua 14:8, 9, 14); at the age of 85 when making this request, Caleb was still going strong. He insisted, "I'm still as strong today as the day Moses sent me out; I'm just as vigorous" (Joshua 14:11). This inner resiliency is even more remarkable after Caleb was on the losing end of a vote that ended badly for Israel for the next 40 years. He could have lingered on the past, brooding about a decision that should have gone the other way. He could have allowed his life to shrink a bit smaller when Joshua was promoted and went on to great things while nothing more is said of Caleb. Caleb had neither of these responses; because he maintained a wholehearted approach to life, he was ready to seize his opportunity when it arose.

This passage suggests that Caleb's final years were among his best—he was still in his "prime of life" at the age of 85, rather than considering himself "over the hill." General Douglas MacArthur touched on the importance of our approach to life, noting:

> "Youth is not a period of time. It is a statement of mind . . . A man doesn't grow old because he has lived a certain number of years. A man grows old when he deserts his ideal. The years may wrinkle his skin, but deserting his ideal wrinkles his soul."

Living wholeheartedly goes hand in hand with finishing well. It positions us to respond well to God's divine opportunities that we'll explore in the next chapter. It also enables us to better live into poet Robert Browning's invitation: "**Grow old along with me! The best is yet to be.**"

Chapter 2

MAKE THE MOST OF YOUR MOMENTS

"I am a little pencil in the hand of a writing God who is sending a love letter to the world."
—Mother Teresa

A pastor was pondering one Sunday morning how to ask his congregation for money to cover an unexpected expense. He was annoyed, therefore, to learn that someone was filling in for the organist, who was ill. When the substitute asked what songs to play, the pastor impatiently passed along a copy of the service and said she would need to add something following his request for additional giving.

Near the end of the service the pastor announced, "Friends, our roof repairs were $5,000 more than expected, and we're in a difficult position. To cover this expense, I'm asking anyone willing to contribute an additional $250 to please stand up." At that moment, the organist began playing *The Star-Spangled Banner*. And that's how the substitute organist became the permanent organist!

Each day provides moments of opportunity, though we won't notice all of them and won't always respond to those we do recognize. Some moments may involve big, life-changing decisions; most, however, are simpler invitations to enter into another's life with a loving smile, an encouraging word, or a helpful gesture. Honoring a wedding vow by caring for a spouse in declining health creates moments of challenge and sacrifice. Asking how someone is doing and waiting for the answer becomes a valuing moment. Sacred moments occur when we choose God's desires over our own.

Finishing well is impacted by how open we are to making the most of moments when they arise. Though we often won't realize it at the time, our response can enlarge or shrink our lives in small but significant ways. These moments present us with a choice of remaining focused upon ourselves or becoming others-focused; the latter provides blessing, enlarges our capacity within, and glorifies God with our faithful response. Author Edward Hale touched upon this choice, writing, "I am only one, but still I am one; I cannot do everything, but still I can do something; and because I cannot do everything, I will not refuse to do the something that I can do."

The good news is that our capacity to make the most of each day's opportunities doesn't diminish with age; we may actually respond better than when we were younger. Consider this observation by John Ortberg: "Love and hurry are fundamentally incompatible. Love always takes time, and time is one thing hurried people don't have." But time is something we *do* have more of once the busyness of a career or raising a family are behind us. Greater space during retirement years results in greater availability to opportunities that God places along our path.

Yes, it can sometimes feel overwhelming to see more needs than we can address—but this chapter is about daily opportunities that we *can* respond to. For as artist Vincent van Gogh remarked, **"The more I think it over, the more I feel that there is nothing more truly artistic than to love people."** Our next story of Esther offers an example of one who made the most of her moment.

Make the Most of Your Moments

Esther's Story

The Old Testament book of Esther is unique in several ways. It and Song of Songs are the only books in the Bible containing no specific mention of God; Esther is also one of only two books (Ruth is the other) named after a woman. Esther offers no biblical instruction for following God. It provides neither direct revelation of His character nor prophetic words that confront behavior or anticipate the Lord's future work. What the book of Esther does have is drama. Though God isn't mentioned specifically by name, we glimpse His activity behind the scenes, placing two individuals in key roles, then using them to save His people. The book of Esther reveals God's preparation for moments of opportunity, even when His presence and activity aren't immediately noticeable.

Esther was a Jewish orphan raised by her cousin Mordecai during the fifth-century B.C.; both were part of the Jewish community that remained in Persia following their exile there. The book begins with King Xerxes summoning Queen Vashti to display her beauty to his guests; when his wife refused, she was stripped of her royal position. One benefit to being king is getting to make the rules—so Xerxes held a beauty contest to select his next queen. The winner was Esther; while her beauty elevated her to this position, the remaining story reveals that she had far more going for her than just looks.

After Esther became queen, Mordecai discovered a plot against the king, and his information led to the capture of those involved. A few years later, Mordecai refused to kneel and honor a nobleman named Haman. Enraged by this lack of respect, Haman sought to destroy not only Mordecai, but every Jew in Persia. Learning of this plan, Mordecai asked Esther to intercede for their people with Xerxes. Esther initially balked because she lacked daily access to the king—anyone approaching Xerxes uninvited was put to death if the king didn't desire that interaction. This hesitation prompted Mordecai to challenge Esther:

> "Do not think that because you are in the king's house you alone of all the Jews will escape. For if you remain silent at this time, relief and deliverance for the Jews will arise from another place, but you and your father's family will perish. And who knows but that you have come to royal position for such a time as this?" (Esther 4:12-14)

Some of sport's most stirring moments occur when weaker competitors come from behind to upset superior opponents. Inspiring as these comebacks are, they have nothing on the abrupt turnaround following Mordecai's challenge to Esther. She found the courage to approach the king, who was pleased to see Esther and offered to grant her wish. After Esther deferred her request to the following day, Xerxes couldn't sleep that night and had the record of his reign read to him. Learning of Mordecai's role in thwarting a plot against him, Xerxes ordered Haman the next day to publically honor Mordecai, the very man he was trying to destroy. Immediately after Haman did so, Esther informed Xerxes of Haman's plan to destroy her people. Xerxes sided with Esther, and Haman was hanged on the gallows he had built for Mordecai. Mordecai was elevated to authority only below the king's. The Jewish people were saved and their enemies destroyed. Whew! This dramatic turnaround occurred because a young woman faithfully responded to the moment God placed before her.

Our Story
During my senior year of college, I participated in a weekly men's

discipleship group led by a professor. That experience transformed my relationship with God by awakening within me a longing to grow spiritually. It prompted a desire to teach others about the Christian faith, which eventually led to ordained ministry. I even added a minor degree in Christian Education during my final two quarters of college. I've always been grateful for the formative depth and commitment that I shared with these men. And I smile to think it was a small, ordinary moment that led to this life-changing experience.

This moment occurred near the end of my junior year, when I sensed a growing desire to participate in a discipleship experience that I'd heard about through friends. It was a surprising inclination because I'd never taken a class from Dr. Edward Smyth, the professor who annually selected a group of male students to disciple—in fact, I'd never even met him. Learning that participation was by invitation only, I scheduled an appointment with the man I later came to know simply as Ed, introduced myself, and asked to be included. Ed could have easily declined my request because he didn't know me—but he promised to pray about it, and I eventually received the desired invitation. I marvel today at how the Lord changed my life through this bold moment of stepping into a new experience led by someone I didn't know.

Many of our moments won't be as life-changing as this one. Then again, I didn't know that my initiative with Ed would have such a significant consequence. Nor could Jesus' disciples anticipate how responding to Christ's invitation to follow Him would change their lives. We never know whether opportunities God places before us will result in significant or inconsequential experiences; we're simply invited to say *yes*. Doing so positions us to experience God's divine purpose for that moment. For this reason, a paraphrase of

Mordecai's words to Esther applies to us today: "Who knows but that you have (been placed in a certain) position for such a time as this?"

Esther's faithful response models three actions that can instruct our moments.

1. Look

The ancient Greeks used two different words for time: *chronos* and *kairos*. As you might guess, *chronos* refers to chronological time of seconds, minutes, or days—time that's measured. In contrast, *kairos* refers to opportunities unmeasured by time, that occur in timely moments. A wedding ceremony is a *chronos* moment on the calendar, prompted by the *kairos* moment of a marriage proposal at an opportune time. *Chronos* represents meeting appointments on our calendars; *kairos* represents divine appointments in our lives. The Apostle Paul used the word *kairos* when he urged us to "make the most of every opportunity" (Ephesians 5:16).

Esther's story centered around a *kairos* moment for which God uniquely positioned this young queen. God does the same with us; the key is to recognize and become responsive to these moments. Don't underestimate the difficulty of this, for two reasons. First, a preoccupation with our needs prompts us to overlook moments God places before us. This was illustrated years ago by two researchers who conducted an experiment at Princeton Seminary. Forty students were instructed to walk to a nearby building and give an impromptu talk. Some were told to talk about the parable of the Good Samaritan, and others about career concerns. Unknown to the students, an actor was planted along their pathway; as each student approached, he groaned and fell to the ground. Sixty percent of these students were so focused on their upcoming presentation, they walked past this person on the ground. Some assigned to talk about the Good Samaritan literally stepped over the actor's body!

We also miss God's *kairos* moments when we overlook those around us. Too often we only see the functional role of others—a waitress who serves us, a neighbor who annoys us, or a friend who shares interests with us. Author Frederick Buechner noted, "**If we are to love our neighbors, before doing anything else we must see our neighbors . . . we must see not just their faces but the life behind and within their faces.**" Looking more intently at others along our path enhances our awareness of opportunities to provide affirmation, encouragement, or comfort. I experienced this recently at a restaurant. Noting that our waiter seemed a bit overwhelmed, I asked his name. When his face instantly lit up, I realized that noticing more than simply his service role prompted him to feel a little more valued. I also recognized that this was a moment I could easily have missed, as I too often do.

Barbara Brown Taylor wrote, "The practice of paying attention is as simple as looking twice at people and things you might just as easily ignore." Esther's moment began when she *looked*; after hearing that Mordecai was mourning in sackcloth, she wanted to know why. Because Esther couldn't leave the palace grounds and Mordecai couldn't approach her, she sent a trusted servant to look and to learn why he was so troubled. Only when Esther made this effort to understand did she learn of the danger facing her people and discover her unique opportunity to do something about it. The more we look for each day's opportunities, the more likely we'll make the most of them. Conversely, less intentional looking often results in missed moments—as the following example illustrates.

In 2005, an elderly man died in Melbourne, Australia while sitting in his parked car. The man remained that way for several days before his death was noticed. Incredibly, a police officer gave the deceased man a parking ticket during this time, attaching it to the windshield of his car! When apologizing, the officer's superior noted, "It is simply a case of the parking officer not noticing."

What can help increase your attentiveness to others along your daily path?

2. Initiate

A man was walking on a beach filled with starfish washed ashore by a high tide, and noticed a young boy throwing them back into the ocean, one by one. When the man asked what he was doing, the boy answered that he was saving the starfish. The man noted that there were thousands on the beach and asked how he hoped to make a difference. The boy picked up a starfish, threw it into the ocean, and replied, "It made a difference for that one." After thinking about his words for a moment, the man joined him in throwing them back.

Noticing moments of need and opportunity is important, but initiative is the fruit of our attentiveness, moving us from our world into the lives of others. However, initiative also introduces uncertainty. Though we may desire to make the most of opportunities God places before us, their unknown cost influences the equation of our responsiveness. Ruth Haley Barton wrote of this cost, "Love is a major inconvenience at times. It . . . challenges my self-centeredness, and sometimes it requires me to give more of myself than I want to give. Sometimes love hurts, or at least it makes me vulnerable. All the time, love is risky, and there are no guarantees."

Esther's opportunity to *initiate* created a dilemma: it required her to literally put her life on the line by approaching the king. This risk led to hesitation—and Esther could have missed her moment if not for Mordecai's urging. Our risk will probably never be as great as Esther's—but risk still feels like risk and can tempt us to hold back from opportunities along our path. Helping someone could make us late for another commitment. Or a moment's demands might require more than we would prefer to give. Henri Nouwen explained the challenge of responding to others' needs:

"Let us not underestimate how hard it is to be compassionate. Compassion is hard because it requires the inner disposition to go with others to the place where they are weak, vulnerable, lonely, and broken. But this is not our spontaneous response to suffering. What we desire most is to do away with suffering by fleeing from it or finding a quick cure for it."

God's *kairos* moments force us to choose between guarding our needs and convenience or taking initiative without fully knowing what will be required of us. Our response to these divine opportunities can impact us every bit as much as those on the receiving end. Israel's two largest bodies of water provide a perfect example. The Sea of Galilee is actually a large lake, fed by water from nearby mountains. Its outflow to the south becomes the Jordan River, which continues until reaching the Dead Sea. The flow of water into and out of the Sea of Galilee leaves it full of life (thus, all the fishermen we read about in the Gospels). But because water only flows into and not out of the Dead Sea, that body of water contains no life—only a growing mineral accumulation.

Moments before us provide more than opportunities to make a difference in the lives of others; they're also opportunities for God to create something new within us. When my morning focus is on getting through responsibilities, the day before me can feel small. But it becomes bigger when my goal is to bless others along my path. Saying "Yes" to daily moments can become a catalyst for deeper life engagement.

What tends to hold you back (cost, fear, etc.) from entering the lives of others?

3. Pray

Prayer was an essential element of Esther's moment; before approaching Xerxes, she asked Mordecai and other Jews to pray for that encounter. Prayer is equally important in making the most of our moments. We ask God's help in the morning to recognize opportunities and to have courage in responding to them. We seek His perspective in the evening to understand moments we missed, and why; we also celebrate faithful moments that the Lord reveals. When love feels lacking in our responses, prayer invites God to enlarge our hearts with an increased capacity and willingness to love.

Esther's big moment can be hard to relate to; after all, the fate of an entire people depended upon her. Conversely, our opportunities will usually occur in smaller moments that seem to make less difference. Remember, though: God can do significant things in moments that seem ordinary to us. Additionally, we often won't know when what seems like a small moment to us may be very big for someone else. Mother Teresa famously observed, "**We cannot do great things in this world, we can only do little things with great love.**" Even when opportunities seem small, we'll never know when a faithful response is preparing us for later bigger moments.

Chick-fil-A founder Truett Cathy described the opportunity of our moments when he asked how to identify someone needing encouragement. His answer: "That person is breathing." We finish well when we recognize fellow travelers along our path, seek to bless them in response—and discover our lives becoming a little bigger as a result.

What's one way you can pray about God's *kairos* moments in your day?

<u>**Final Thought**</u>
The poem, *Things You Didn't Do*, was submitted to speaker and author Leo Buscaglia by a college student during his teaching career:

Remember the day I borrowed your brand new car and I dented it?

I thought you'd kill me, but you didn't.

And remember the time I dragged you to the beach, and you said it would rain, and it did?

I thought you'd say, "I told you so." But you didn't.

Do you remember the time I flirted with all the guys to make you jealous, and you were?

I thought you'd leave me, but you didn't.

Do you remember the time I spilled strawberry pie all over your car rug?

I thought you'd hit me, but you didn't.

And remember the time I forgot to tell you the dance was formal and you showed up in jeans?

I thought you'd drop me, but you didn't.

Yes, there were lots of things you didn't do.

But you put up with me, and you loved me, and you protected me.

There were lots of things I wanted to make up to you when you returned from Viet Nam.

But you didn't.

God places divine moments before us each day that linger only for a time before they're gone. The Lord encourages us to look for

His *kairos* opportunities, take initiative into others' lives, and seek His help in making the most of our moments. Faithfully stringing these moments together can result in a life of great impact—which we'll consider in our next chapter.

Chapter 3

LEAVE BEHIND SOMETHING OF YOURSELF

"The measure of a life is not its duration but its donation."
—Corrie ten Boom

Pastor Wayne Cordeiro wrote in *Doing Church as a Team* of a rabbi in Russia during the nineteenth century. Discouraged by a lack of purpose and direction and questioning his faith in God and call to ministry, the rabbi wandered one night through the empty city streets. Caught up in despair, he unknowingly entered a Russian military compound that was off-limits to civilians. Suddenly, a Russian soldier was barking at him, "Who are you, and what are you doing here?"

The rabbi paused for a moment, then asked the solder to repeat his questions. When he did, the rabbi said to the soldier with delight, as if making a great discovery, "I will pay you to ask me those same two questions every day: Who are you, and what are you doing here?"

Who are you, and what are you doing here? We turn from making the most of daily moments to a larger look at what we'll leave behind to show for our years. Rabbi Harold Kushner observed, "I am convinced that it is not the fear of death, of our lives ending, that haunts our sleep so much as the fear that our lives will not have mattered, that as far as the world is concerned, we might as well never have lived." This emerged in a survey of people over the age of 95; when asked what they would have changed, a consistent wish was to have done more that lived on after their death. Philosopher William James summarized this instinct by saying, "**The greatest use of life is to spend it for something that will outlast it.**"

Finishing well occurs when others are blessed by how we've lived. Though our lives are often evaluated by the accomplishments, leisure, and financial security that fill them, these elements rarely contribute to any lasting legacy. Funerals tend to most clearly reveal a life's impact. No matter how much an individual accumulated or how eloquent or tearful the eulogy, the ultimate evidence of lasting value comes from family and friends who believe their lives are better because of that person. Poet Ralph Waldo Emerson captured this when he wrote:

> "To leave the world a bit better
> Whether by a healthy child, a redeemed social condition
> or a job well done;
> To know even one other life has breathed easier because
> you lived:
> This is to have succeeded."

Think of ripples created when a rock is thrown into still water. We want to create impactful ripples that flow outward from our lives and even outlast us. When we were young, such ripples were easily noticed, as our lives expanded with accomplishments and growing circles of influence. As we grow older, we must increasingly have faith that ripples continue flowing from our lives, even if less visibly than they once did. Chapter 11 of the New Testament book of Hebrews describes individuals who remained faithful even when unable to see what was promised by God. Our challenge during later years in life is to create ripples the best we can, trusting that the Lord will use our faithful efforts even when we can't see the results.

Each of us can identify individuals who have impacted our lives. Finishing well results in grateful recipients of what we've left behind. The story of Abram (later known as Abraham) reveals one who longed to leave behind something of himself through a long-elusive descendent.

Abram's Story

Abram was the father of the nation of Israel, fulfilling God's assurance in Genesis 12 that a great nation would arise from his descendants. There was just one problem: at the time of that promise, Abram was 75 years old with no children. It's always devastating when a couple desires children but can't give birth; the pressure to have children in biblical times may have been even greater. Not only were children important to carry on the family name, they were also counted on to populate and maintain a family's land for successive generations. Barrenness was perceived in Old Testament times as a curse or punishment, often resulting in shame. On one occasion, Jacob's wife Rachel declared that she would die if she couldn't give birth (Genesis 30).

Despite God's great promise, Abram and Sarai still had no children by the following conversation with Him in Genesis 15:

> The word of the LORD came to Abram in a vision: "Do not be afraid, Abram. I am your shield, your very great reward."
>
> But Abram said, "Sovereign LORD, what can you give me since I remain childless and the one who will inherit my estate is Eliezer of Damascus?" And Abram said, "You have given me no children; so a servant in my household will be my heir."

Then the word of the LORD came to him: "This man will not be your heir, but a son who is your own flesh and blood will be your heir." He took him outside and said, "Look up at the sky and count the stars—if indeed you can count them." Then he said to him, "So shall your offspring be."

Abram believed the LORD, and he credited it to him as righteousness. (Genesis 15:1-6)

Abram by this time had already experienced much of God's initial promise in chapter 12. He'd accumulated animals and servants (Genesis 12:16), become very wealthy in livestock, silver and gold (Genesis 13:2), and owned all the land he could see in every direction (Genesis 13:14-16). Abram's land and wealth would have been envied by many—but he still lacked one element of God's promise. Abram didn't have an heir who would continue his name and legacy, and all else seemingly paled in comparison.

After all, a child was the only portion of God's promise that Abram attempted to produce himself. It's never hinted that Abram sought to accumulate greater wealth or possessions than he already had. What God provided seemed enough. Abram even allowed his nephew Lot to pick the land he preferred, and Abram took what remained (Genesis 13). But as Abram's childlessness continued, we sense a growing desperation. Perhaps God's promise reawakened Abram and Sarai's longing for a child, after they had previously made peace with not having one. After years of waiting for God's promised heir, Abram and Sarai remained childless—so they took matters into their own hands.

We don't know how many days of ache and impatience occurred between God's repeated assurance of descendants in Genesis 15 and their actions at the outset of chapter 16. Abandoning any hope that God would provide the promised heir, Abram and Sarai produced one themselves through Sarai's servant Hagar. Their inability to trust God's promise resulted in great family and geographic conflict after He eventually did give this couple a child. Abram's longing for an heir through whom he could leave behind something of himself made his obedience even more remarkable in Genesis 22, when God tested him with instructions to sacrifice the son that He'd provided. Abram desired an heir who would continue his name, but his love for God in that moment was even greater.

Our Story

Writing these words on Father's Day reminded me of a parent's role in passing values, family history, and life competencies along to the next generation. Like Abram who longed for a son to become a lasting extension of his life, we desire to leave behind something from our lives that impacts others. An example of this occurred one morning at a drive-through coffee lane in Portland, Oregon. A woman decided to pay not only for her coffee, but for the coffee of the person in the car behind her. When the next customer was informed of this, he responded by purchasing coffee for the next person behind him. Incredibly, this generosity continued for 25 more customers, each paying for the next (makes you wonder who the Grinch was who ended the process). These actions illustrate the ripple that we seek to create.

We may also share a second similarity with Abram. Contributing something that lingers after we're gone may feel as unlikely to us as having a child did to him. Three factors can dampen our hope of leaving behind something of ourselves—but there's also an encouraging way to think about each.

- **Ordinary lives**

A building or street won't be named for most of us. We'll probably also lack societal contributions that outlive us, such as a cure for cancer. Any lasting ripple from our lives will most likely come from how we've poured into people. Author Dave Peterson stated, "The longest enduring legacy you can leave with your life is the way you bless others."

Fortunately, even ordinary lives have great potential to bless others. The principle of compounded interest allows small amounts of money to gradually grow over time into larger amounts. Ordinary days have the same potential to compound with time. Novelist Anne Dillard reinforced this when she wrote, "**How you spend your days is, of course, how you spend your life.**" Compounded interest from ordinary day after ordinary day of blessing others can result in ripples that continue after we're gone.

- **Older lives**

As our years increase, so does the likelihood that much of our life's contribution has already been made. This is true of my role as parent; my primary influence upon Matthew and Suzanne, both in their twenties, now lies more in the past than the future. Yet we dare not allow what's already behind us to limit our impact upon what's still before us. Though our remaining years are steadily decreasing, what's left can still create ripples.

Leadership guru Peter Drucker shared an experience that raises an important question:

> "When I was thirteen, I had an inspiring teacher of religion who one day went right through the class of boys asking each one, 'What do you want to be remembered for?'

None of us, of course, could give an answer. So, he chuckled and said, 'I didn't expect you to be able to answer it. But if you still can't answer it by the time you're fifty, you will have wasted your life.' We eventually had a sixtieth reunion of that high school class. (At one point) one of the fellows asked, 'Do you remember Father Pfliegler and that question?' We all remembered it. And each one said it had made all the difference to him.

I'm always asking that question: 'What do you want to be remembered for?' It is a question that induces you to renew yourself, because it pushes you to see yourself as a different person—the person you can become."

What do you want to be remembered for? Regardless of current age and previous impact, how we answer this question in the years ahead will influence the ripple that we're still creating.

- **Limited lives**

As we grow older, it becomes easier to dwell more upon what we cannot do than what we still can. Activities we once enjoyed may no longer be possible. Perhaps distance prevents us from spending as much time with friends or family members as we'd like. At some point we're slowed by less energy and resiliency. These and other limitations can make us question whether we still have the capacity to leave behind something of ourselves.

Limitations can be a hard ceiling to push against, but they're really nothing new; limitations have always been part of life. During our early years, we chaffed against restrictions from enjoying certain activities because we weren't old enough. Later, establishing a career and/or family limited our time to do or accomplish all that we wanted to. <u>Limitations in our older years just look different from others we've experienced in the past.</u> Whatever our limitations today, there's still much we *can* do to create ripples. As my former Senior Pastor, John Stevens, once encouraged our older adults, "We need to focus on what we can do and do have rather than on what we used to be able to do or have lost." I also like the wisdom attributed to Betty Reese: "If you think you are too small to make a difference, you have never been in bed with a mosquito!"

These and other factors may tempt us to assume that we're no longer leaving behind much from our lives. Don't believe it! Speaker Juliet Funt offered this wonderful encouragement about our potential to still create ripples: **"A legacy is a story about you that is yet to be written, but for which you hold the pen."**

With this perspective in mind, let's briefly explore six actions that can help us leave behind more of our legacy.

1. Assess—And Celebrate!
The fertile field of opportunity before us is important—but let's not lose sight of seeds previously planted. Since we've already lived a large percentage of our lives, we have a large canvas from which to identify and celebrate where we've blessed and been appreciated by others. Though we don't want to rest on past accomplishments, it can be encouraging to recognize ways in which we've already left behind something of ourselves.

As we assess where and when ripples have flowed from our lives, it may be helpful to break our years into decades and to think of relationships and activity during each of these segments. Even then, potential ripples may be difficult to identify, especially as we move apart from others in distance and relationship. Making a short list of those we've been closest to over the years may help provide some definition; so can reaching out to some on our list, asking them to share how we touched their lives. This project could even provide a mutual blessing if we first share our gratitude for their ripple into our life.

Who can you identify that you've poured into and impacted over the years?

2. Offer Words of Blessing

A doctor frequently at the bedside of dying patients shared the phrases that they most frequently longed to hear: *"I'll miss you,"* *"Thank you,"* *"I forgive you,"* and *"I love you."* Each phrase was important because it affirmed the recipient's value; together, they illustrate the power of our words to create ripples into others' lives.

As we think of friends and family most important to us, are there any from whom we've unintentionally withheld words of encouragement? When did they last hear us say we love them—or more specifically, what we're proud of or admire about them? We've undoubtedly done this over the years—but has it been awhile since we've offered fresh words that enhance our ripple of blessing into the lives of these individuals?

How can you bless someone with your words this week?

3. Find a Need and Meet It

Looking for ways to meet the needs of others doesn't bless only those recipients; it also becomes redemptive for us. A focus upon others nudges us away from a natural inclination to make life about us. Initiative into the lives of others reinforces that we still have something to offer the world; plus, there's an added benefit for us. According to *Time* magazine, "doing volunteer work—in such places as hospitals and soup kitchens that allow direct contact with the people you're helping—may lower mortality rates by as much as 22% compared with those of non-volunteers."

Years ago, I led our church's Divorce Recovery Workshop. Hundreds of men and women annually attended this workshop, each processing the painful ending of a marriage that they thought would last forever. It was always inspiring to watch dozens of workshop participants return months later to walk alongside the next group of hurting people who attended. These men and women allowed an unwanted and devastating experience to become an opportunity to impact others going through the same thing. I also find inspiration from my 88-year-old mother, who sings in her church choir and occasionally plays the piano for worship, makes quilts and knits stocking caps for those less fortunate, and prays. Finally, I think of those in the Sunday class I teach who joyfully volunteer in our church's preschool, or generously give time and resources to other organizations.

If you haven't seen the animated movie *Up*, I highly recommend it. (The opening scenes alone, of a couple growing old together will tug at your heart.) Throughout the movie, 78-year-old Carl is too focused upon his needs to pay attention to a young, fatherless boy named Russell who's starving for attention. By the end of the movie, Carl's willingness to pour into Russell results in blessing for both. The same can be true for us, as we share with others what we still can contribute.

What experience has God uniquely placed in your life that can be of help to others?

4. Pass Along Memories

You may be your family's oldest remaining source of memories, but are rarely asked about them. Family memories are often unvalued until questions of the past arise that no one is left to answer. Because of this, it can be helpful to anticipate information that family members may one day desire and record your memories. Unique family stories or accomplishments might interest some; family trees can also provide historical context. Pictures tell wonderful stories of previous chapters in family members' lives. When my mom recently moved, she gave me pictures and other items that she could no longer keep. Among the memories that I most treasured: a picture of my parents when they were engaged; the bill for my birth ($166.24, and I was worth every penny); and a picture of my grandmother on her high school tennis team (something I hadn't known about her).

Recording memories in written form allows them to outlast us. Audio recordings can add another layer of blessing, allowing others to hear our voice after we're gone. I remember my delight years ago when listening to an old family recording of my dad speaking when he was a teenager, hearing for the first time what he sounded like at that age.

Our story is also an important part of the next generation's story after us—and they'll also value it some day. Yes, any gift of memories may initially be put to one side by recipients too busy for them right now. But one day, when there's time and inclination to learn more about family heritage, what we've taken the time to pass along could provide great blessing that outlasts our years here on earth.

How can you preserve or even share some of your memories with loved ones?

5. Give Grace

This step may not be for everyone, but the discouraging reality is that we sometimes don't see a particular ripple from our lives that we longed for. Perhaps children haven't caught the values or life skills that we've sought to pass along. Maybe we poured into a marriage or business that didn't go as we'd hoped. These experiences are always disappointing, but we need not allow this lack of perceived ripples to define our entire legacy. Yes, our lives may not have the impact in places where we'd hoped they would—but let's not discount other areas of life where we *have* made a lasting difference.

Where do you feel disappointment from longed-for ripples that haven't occurred?

6. Pray

Prayer could have been our first listed action and perhaps should have been, given the impact that prayers can have. It's listed last because it's the one thing we can all do even if the other five suggestions for leaving behind something of ourselves feel too elusive. Prayers become our greatest contribution to others, for they invite God to do for them what we cannot. Throughout my lifetime, my parents have offered countless prayers for me and for my family; I'm convinced that much of what I've experienced and enjoyed in life is due to those prayers.

The power of our silent, hidden prayers to ripple into others' lives highlights an important truth about leaving behind something of ourselves: our life's impact will sometimes go unnoticed by us or uncredited by others. And that's ok. Mahatma Gandhi once stated:

> "It's the action, not the fruit of the action, that's important. You have to do the right thing. It may not be in your power, may not be in your time, that there'll be any fruit. But that doesn't mean you stop doing the right thing. You may never know what results come from your action. But if you do nothing, there will be no result."

Who are you regularly praying for?
The story behind the Washington Monument in our nation's

capital illustrates our potential to miss seeing the ripples we create. Architect Robert Mills' proposal of a 555-foot high granite obelisk to honor the nation's first president was approved by the Washington National Monument Society in 1836. Unfortunately, numerous delays and challenges slowed its progress over the next 19 years. When Mills died in 1855, construction had come to a complete standstill, with only a 150-foot stump to show for his dream. It took Congress another 25 years to finally fund and build this monument as Mills envisioned. The Washington Monument was a tangible contribution left behind from Mills' life—he just didn't get to see it.

Final Thought

This story by motivational speaker Helice Bridges illustrates our impact upon others:

A teacher in New York decided to honor her high school seniors. First, she told each how they made a difference to her and to the class. Then she presented each with a blue ribbon imprinted with gold letters, which read, "Who I Am Makes A Difference."

Afterwards, she decided to do a class project. She gave each student three more ribbons and instructed them to spread this acknowledgment ceremony. Then they were to follow up on the results and report back to the class.

One student honored a junior executive in a nearby company for helping him with his career planning. The student put the blue ribbon on his shirt, then passed along the two extra ribbons and asked him to find someone else to honor, then ask that person to acknowledge a third person with the extra blue ribbon and report back what happened.

Later that day the junior executive approached his boss and told him that he admired him for being a creative genius. The junior executive asked if he would accept the gift of the blue ribbon, and was given permission to place it on his boss's jacket. He then asked if his boss would support the class project by passing along the final ribbon and reporting back.

That night the boss sat down with his 14-year old son and said, "The most incredible thing happened to me today. One of the junior executives came in and told me he admired me and gave me a blue ribbon for being a creative genius. He then gave me an extra one and asked me to find someone else to honor.

"As I was driving home tonight, I started thinking about whom I would honor with this ribbon, and I thought about you. I want to honor you. My days are really hectic and when I come home I don't pay a lot of attention to you. Sometimes I scream at you for not getting good enough grades in school and for your bedroom being a mess. But tonight I just wanted to let you know that you do make a difference to me. Besides your mother, you are the most important person in my life. You're a great kid and I love you!"

The startled boy began to sob, and couldn't stop crying. He finally looked up at his father and said through his tears, "I was planning to commit suicide tonight because I didn't think you cared. Now I don't need to."

We've all been touched by others who entered our lives and left us better because of their influence. As we seek to finish well, let's consider how we can leave behind something of ourselves that creates ripples into the lives of others. Our next chapter explores the relationships where this impact will often occur.

Chapter 4

LEAN UPON OTHERS

"The yearning to attach and connect, to love and be loved, is the fiercest longing of the soul. Our need for community with people and the God who made us is to the human spirit what food and air and water are to the human body."
—John Ortberg

My wife Deborah and I honeymooned in Hawaii 29 years ago. During breakfast our final morning, I noticed someone staring at us from across the restaurant. I reactively stared back—and quickly realized that the other person was a friend from seminary. After introductions with Chris and his wife Linda, we discovered that the four of us were flying home on the same plane that afternoon. We reconnected again later at the airport; Deborah and Linda began a conversation while Chris and I caught up on the previous three years. At one point Chris shared that they had anticipated the birth of their first child the previous year, but Linda had miscarried. Describing their emotions during that loss, Chris said something I've never forgotten: "I never knew until that moment how little I really knew my wife."

When God created us in His image, He placed within each of us His own relational nature. Knowing and being known by others on a deep level isn't optional—it's how we're wired. The 1980s television show *Cheers* touched on this relational need with its opening song lyrics: "*Sometimes you want to go where everybody knows your name, and they're always glad you came.*" We're most fully alive when known by others not only in name, but for who we really are: our hopes, our dreams, our aches, and our fears. Rick Warren reinforced the importance of this:

> "Often we act as if relationships are something to be squeezed into our schedule. We talk about finding time for our children or making time for people in our lives. That gives the impression that relationships are just a part of our lives along with many other tasks. But **God says relationships are what life is all about.**"

Finishing well is enhanced when our journey is shared with others. During our early years, the circle of those who know us expands from neighborhood friends to classmates at school, then later professional, church, and social relationships. But this circle of meaningful relationships gradually contracts later in life when we retire from a job and lose its accompanying social interactions. We also begin losing close friends and family to death, are separated by physical relocation, or experience more limited social mobility. Studies verify that as people grow older, they interact with fewer people. As our circle of friends shrinks, we may question whether the effort required to rebuild it again is worth it. Allowing our social network to diminish, though, risks experiencing less than God's best for us relationally. As Greek Philosopher Epicurus once said, "Of all the means to ensure happiness throughout the whole life, by far the most important is the acquisition of friends."

Who knows you best today? Is your circle of friends increasing or decreasing?

Our next story of Moses reveals one who understood his need to lean relationally upon others, and the benefit of doing so.

Moses' Story

When we think of Moses, we tend to picture solitary, towering, Charlton Heston-like moments: staring down Pharaoh in the battle over Israel's freedom; stretching out his hand to part the Red Sea; receiving God's 10 commandments on Mt. Sinai; or steady leadership of a people who often didn't want to be wherever they were. Moses seems bigger than life in these and other moments. Though often accompanied by others, he usually did the heavy lifting.

But the next story is different; it provides a glimpse of Moses' need for others. Moses capably addressed each challenge before this moment, from the Israelites' dramatic Red Sea escape to repeated needs for water and food in the desert. Now a new crisis arose: the Israelites were threatened by the Amalekites, following years of slavery that hadn't prepared them to defend themselves. Once again, something was required of Moses—but this time he had to rely upon others:

> The Amalekites came and attacked the Israelites at Rephidim. Moses said to Joshua, "Choose some of our men and go out to fight the Amalekites. Tomorrow I will stand on top of the hill with the staff of God in my hands."
>
> So Joshua fought the Amalekites as Moses had ordered, and Moses, Aaron and Hur went to the top of the hill. As long as Moses held up his hands, the Israelites were winning, but whenever he lowered his hands, the Amalekites were winning. When Moses' hands grew tired, they took a stone and put it under him and he sat on it. Aaron and Hur held his hands up—one on one side, one on the other—so

that his hands remained steady till sunset. So Joshua overcame the Amalekite army with the sword. (Exodus 17:8-13)

Moses assured the Israelites that the staff in his hands would be a
visual reminder of God's provision in battle; while he held it up, they
would prevail. That provided the encouragement his countrymen
needed for this new challenge. But Moses understood he couldn't
do this by himself, and that he needed to lean upon others. Moses
didn't even try to initially pull this off alone. Before walking up the
hill, Moses asked two men whom he trusted—his brother Aaron
and another man named Hur—to join him. This wasn't a private
request; Moses was publicly acknowledging his dependence upon
them. In the hours that followed, Moses' arms and legs tired, as
he knew they would. But these two men men placed a rock under
Moses when he needed to sit and held up his arms when he grew
tired of holding his staff. When the Israelites looked up the hill that
day, they didn't see a leader who could handle things on his own;
instead, they saw Moses' need for others to accomplish what was
required of him. Moses wasn't too proud to admit that he couldn't
do it alone.

This story provides the first of two back-to-back acknowledge-
ments by Moses of his need to lean upon others. After it concludes
chapter 17 of Exodus, chapter 18 begins with a visit from Moses'
father-in-law, Jethro. Jethro quickly perceived that Moses was in
an unsustainable role, serving as judge for everyone the entire day.
This unending responsibility may be why Moses previously sent
away his wife and children (Exodus 18:2). Jethro wisely noted that
Moses couldn't do this by himself, declaring, "What you are doing
is not good. You and these people who come to you will only wear
yourselves out. The work is too heavy for you; you cannot handle it

alone" (Exodus 18:17-18). Jethro suggested that Moses select others to share the weight of this responsibility. Moses wisely listened to his father-in-law, and the Israelites again witnessed their leader's willingness to lean upon others. Moses' example can encourage us to do the same.

<u>Our Story</u>

Dallas Willard noted, **"The natural condition of life for human beings is one of reciprocal rootedness in others."** Legos were among our children's favorite toys when they were young and offer a great example of God placing a need within each of us for reciprocal rootedness. These assorted plastic pieces weren't created to exist alone; each has notches on the top and holes on the bottom for the specific purpose of connecting with other Legos. One piece by itself isn't much to look at; combined with others, beautiful works of art can be created.

When his favorite college professor was dying of ALS, Mitch Albom began spending Tuesdays at his bedside. Albom's book, *Tuesdays with Morrie*, describes this experience and his mentor's wisdom during these times together. On one occasion Morrie told Albom, "In the beginning of life, when we're infants, we need each other, right? At the end of life when you get like me, we need each other, right? Well Mitch, here's the secret: in between we need each other as well."

Just as Moses was physically supported by Aaron and Hur, we need the social, emotional and spiritual support of others. When we experience loss or pain, the presence and encouragement of friends provides reinforcement and perspective. In moments when our faith in God feels thin, we can lean upon another's faith without being judged. Friends also provide helpful correction when we head down questionable paths or make choices not in our best interest. Proverbs 27:17 declares, "As iron sharpens iron, so one person sharpens another."

A recent *Wall Street Journal* article touched upon our created need for each other by noting the loneliness of older Americans:

> "Researchers have found that loneliness takes a physical toll, and is as closely linked to early mortality as smoking up to 15 cigarettes a day or consuming more than six alcoholic drinks a day. Loneliness is even worse for longevity than being obese or physically inactive."

The same article referenced a review of 148 independent studies on loneliness from more than 300,000 participants; the review concluded that increased social connection reduced the risk of early death by half. Noting similar research, John Ortberg concluded, "In other words, it is better to eat Twinkies with good friends than to eat broccoli alone!"

Even when we sense benefit to new friendships, we're often hesitant to reach out; after all, we're never certain at any relationship's outset whether the time developing it will be worth it. For this reason, we can be tempted to spend our time on activities rather than people. But remember that we're created for relationships—which means that who we're with will provide more lasting meaning over the long run than what we do. Too many times, I interact with individuals experiencing a crisis by themselves because they hadn't done the work of building community in advance. Conversely, those I admire most give themselves away generously to others.

Developing new friendships to fill the void of those we lose is admittedly time-consuming and challenging. Let's look at five ways we can develop and maintain a meaningful circle of friendships to lean upon.

1. Take Initiative

After moving to Southern California to attend seminary, I started worshiping on Sundays at a large nearby church. Though the church offered many opportunities to develop community, I chose to only attend worship. I enjoyed the services each week, slipping in by myself, sitting near the front, then slipping out again at the end. After some months of this pattern, I found myself thinking one week during worship, "If I didn't return next Sunday, would anyone notice?" I realized that no one would—and I didn't go back the next week. I eventually found another church, and this time tried at the outset to know others with whom I worshiped.

This experience taught me that comfortable but isolating habits often fail to satisfy in the long run. I now tell people that though worship may draw them to a church, it's relationships that will keep them coming back over time. But relationships require work. We tend to approach new relationships like visitors approach Disneyland, thinking we can experience it just by showing up. However, relationships are more like a child's Christmas gift: some assembly is required. The beginning of this assembly work is the initiative we take to enter into others' lives.

We sometimes hesitate to initiate because we risk non-reciprocation. If this fear is reinforced by previous experience, we can develop a protective posture that retreats at any sign of rejection, like a turtle withdrawing into its shell. Though that's a safe response, it often causes us to miss out on the relationships we desire and for which God created us.

My relational circle has been small for most of my life. I'm still years from retirement but am starting to think more about the social connections I'll need when work relationships no longer fill my day. I'm realizing that I need to exert additional relational effort now if I want to enjoy meaningful friendships during later years. Even when our initiative doesn't result in a lasting connection, we're exercising relational muscles that help with the next person.

Toward whom would you like to take a first relational step? How will you do so?

2. Peel, Don't Polish

In *Why Am I Afraid to Tell You Who I Am?* author John Powell provided the following answer: "I'm afraid to tell you who I am because if I tell you who I am, you might not like who I am. And that's all I have." Deep within each of us, to varying degrees, is a fear that others might retreat from us if they better understood who we really are. For this reason, we limit what we share of ourselves; however, this guardedness hinders intimacy with others and can be wearying for us. During the original television series *Star Trek*, Captain Kirk and his crew battled Romulans in one episode who possessed a cloaking device that kept their ship invisible. At one point in the battle Kirk observed, "They can't keep it up forever. The cloaking device will soon drain their energy banks." The same is true for us.

Developing new relationships requires revealing to others who we really are. Journalist Sydney Harris noted that while the human personality is like a banana that needs to be peeled, we instinctively polish it like an apple so that others will be drawn to us. **Lasting friendships are formed by peeling away layers that allow others to see and understand us in deeper ways.** Otherwise, we risk never being known for who we really are—as silent film star Charlie Chaplin once experienced.

A contest was held years ago to determine who most looked like Chaplin. Some of Chaplin's closest friends were invited to judge the contestants; unknown to them, he secretly entered the contest. Amazingly, Chaplin finished third in his own look-alike competition! Enlarging our social circle requires a willingness to trust others with who we are. It's usually helpful to begin with safer details about our past, before working up to current experiences or feelings. As sharing with others moves deeper, a principle offered by pastor Mike Platter is helpful.

Platter noted that our home basements are usually off limits from new guests. We initially host them in a tidied-up living room and only bring others into the basement after relationships develop more depth. Platter compared sharing personal information with others to taking people down into our personal basement. Though revealing little about us tends to keep people at a distance, so does revealing too much too quickly. Platter suggested that our healthiest approach is to walk others step by step into the basement of our lives, in sync with their sharing. This is contrary to how many approach today's social media platforms like Facebook, where deeply personal details are shared with a large, non-intimate audience. Relationships are built well when we find the balance between too little and too much sharing.

If you're inclined to hold back from sharing with others, why do you think that is?

3. Ask Others Their Story
We all have life stories that we'd love to tell but are seldom asked about. Since that's also true of those with whom we seek to connect,

asking questions about their lives can often start a conversation. We'll usually receive a positive response from others who are grateful to tell their story—and as we demonstrate interest, they'll hopefully become equally interested in someone so interested in them. Lack of reciprocation may indicate a one-sided and unhealthy focus from which we'll want to move on.

Listening intently isn't easy, though, as author Ben Patterson's story about President Franklin Roosevelt's behavior at a gala ball illustrates:

> Tired of shaking hands and smiling his big smile and saying all of the usual inanities at such occasions, Roosevelt tried doing something outrageous. Convinced that no one was listening anyway, he greeted each person by saying, "I murdered my grandmother this morning." Everyone he met smiled vacuously and said things like: "Wonderful!" "Lovely!" "Keep up the good work!" One diplomat was listening, however. He leaned over and whispered in Roosevelt's ear, "I'm sure she had it coming to her!"

Author Steven Covey suggested why listening to others can be so challenging: "Most people do not listen with the intent to understand; they listen with the intent to reply. They're either speaking or preparing to speak." Asking and listening flow from understanding that relationships aren't just about us, but also what we bring into others' lives. When asking questions, it can be helpful to creatively anticipate information that others would enjoy sharing. The more mutually attentive we are in encouraging and building up each other, the healthier our friendships can become.

Who can you ask questions of this week?

4. Accept Inconvenience

A doctor, attorney, and pastor were on a deserted island together for a long time, when a sealed bottle one day washed ashore. A genie appeared when it was opened and announced that he'd grant each man one wish. The doctor noted that he'd been on the verge of a cure for cancer before he was shipwrecked, and that he'd like to finish his work. He said, "I wish I was home"—and he was gone. The attorney declared that he'd spent a lot of time thinking about helping others during his time on the island; he also had a wife and children whom he missed. After declaring, "I wish I was home," he was also gone.

The pastor looked around his now deserted beach and said, "I really liked those guys. I wish they were still here!"

That's a humorous reminder that relationships can complicate our lives. Sometimes they'll demand time or energy that may already be in short supply. There's also potential for conflict. When friendships are built upon common interests, differing opinions or values can make things uncomfortable. Friendships meaningfully add to our lives but can also be messy—as a three-legged race illustrates.

Whether you've participated in a three-legged race, watched one, or just know this instinctively, two people with their adjacent legs tied together generally won't run as fast as one person alone. As we become more set in our ways of what we like to do and how we like to do it, we more easily believe we're better off on our own than relationally connected with others who might slow us down. No matter how true that feels, remember that we're wired for relationships and experience life best when we're in them. We'll usually discover in the long run that the blessings and benefits of new friendships more than offset any inconvenience.

In what ways do you find relationships inconvenient?

5. Be Patient

New friendships need time to develop. Society increasingly offers opportunities for quick results, such as microwaves or sending text messages. But as author Terry Hershey noted, "**The seeds of a relationship can be planted quickly. The watering, weeding and fertilizing take months and even years.**" We sometimes forget that our most meaningful previous relationships usually didn't develop overnight; they required time and patience before bearing the fruit we enjoyed from them. For that reason, it's wise to avoid comparing previous relationships established over time with today's newer experiences. Let's allow each new relational opportunity the time it needs to develop its own unique character.

It would be great if all our relational efforts were successful—but that's rarely the case. Salespeople know that each successful sale is offset by multiple unsuccessful attempts. It often takes multiple attempts at new friendships before we experience lasting ones. That's neither a statement about us nor those we attempt to connect with—it's simply a fact of life.

Think of a current meaningful friendship; how long did it take to develop what you've enjoyed?

Final Thought

Jimmy Durante was a popular twentieth-century entertainer once asked by Ed Sullivan to perform in a show for World War II veterans. Durante agreed, but stated that he could only entertain for a few minutes before needing to depart for another commitment. When Durante appeared on stage, though, things didn't go as planned. After his initial routine resulted in applause, Durante continued performing much longer than he'd promised. When he finally left the stage, Sullivan expressed gratitude for Durante's lengthier contribution in light of his other commitment.

Durante admitted that he would be late for it. He then told Sullivan that if he looked at the front row, he would understand why Durante felt compelled to stay. In the middle of the row were two men; each had lost an arm during the war, and they were applauding by clapping their two remaining hands together.

That's a beautiful image of our relationships with others. Each of us brings our own sin imperfections and limitations—and then, like disabled servicemen and Lego pieces, we become more through our connection with others than we could ever be on our own. The better we learn to do this, the more rewarding will be our finish.

PART II
LOOKING WITHIN

Chapter 5

LIVE TO YOUR FULL POTENTIAL

"God is always calling us to be more than we have been."
—Loren Mead

I earned my seminary degree 35 years ago with no intention of ever becoming a pastor. I enjoyed learning more about the Bible, and planned to serve within my congregation as a volunteer while working outside the church. Pastoring was so far off my radar, I successfully petitioned out of seminary preaching classes that were required of students with my degree.

I was surprised, therefore, near the end of my classes to sense an inward pull toward working in the church. I quickly dismissed the thought, assuming it was prompted by a desire to remain within a spiritual environment like seminary. After all, I perceived that pastors were far more holy than I would ever be (I now know better). But this internal pull remained, even as I continued resisting it over the next months. One day I finally acknowledged to God, "I think this is from you." Immediately, my tension around this decision disappeared—and I realized the Lord was calling me into one of the last roles I would have ever chosen for myself. But my surprise at God's leading didn't end there.

Nearly 20 years later, I sensed my passion waning for the Singles Ministry that I'd led at our church for 10 years. As I began exploring other ministry positions around the country, our Congregational Care pastor announced her retirement. I'd previously declared to her on numerous occasions, "I would *never* want your job!" The unpredictable and persistent responsiveness to congregational needs that this role required seemed beyond both my capacity and desire. Once again, I was adamant about what I wouldn't do; when our Executive Pastor asked the retiring pastor about my suitability for the position she responded, "John would be perfect—but he'd never take it."

Another internal tug during the following months, accompanied by personal reflection and conversations with those who knew me well, once again moved me into a role that I hadn't foreseen. Today, it's hard to imagine another vocation or pastoral role as meaningful as this one. And I learned from these two experiences to not tell God what I won't do.

Finishing well requires an openness to developing new muscles that use more of who we are. **As we grow older, it's easy to allow what we've previously done to shape our perception of what we still can do.** We're inclined to resist new paths that are different from what we've experienced or understand about ourselves. But looking back over life, many of us were probably surprised to find ourselves at times in different roles than we'd anticipated. That's how God works—He delights in surprising us with new opportunities, rather than simply rubber-stamping what we believe we're up to. For He really does understand what we're capable of, far better than we do.

When were you surprised by an opportunity that you didn't think you were up to?

The Lord's opportunities often expand our capacity for living well and finishing well, even if they initially seem beyond us. For

He already knows what a major study on aging once discovered: older adults are capable of changing their behavior up to the day of their death. Our next story of Gideon provides an example of God's surprising opportunities and encourages a posture of openness to new possibilities.

Gideon's Story
The book of Judges describes a repetitious cycle: God blessed Israel; Israel neglected God; God allowed Israel to experience adversity; Israel turned to God; God blessed Israel . . . and so on. Gideon's story occurred in the twelfth century B.C. during a period of adversity. The Midianites were a nomadic people who invaded and destroyed the land of Israel and other nations. They pillaged Israel's crops and cattle for seven years prior to this story, prompting people to hide in caves. The Midianites were among the first to utilize domesticated camels, which gave them increased mobility and a swift striking capability. We're told that they were "like swarms of locusts," and that "it was impossible to count the men and their camels" (Judges 6:5). So, we can understand why this encounter was so disconcerting for Gideon:

> The angel of the LORD came and sat down under the oak in Ophrah that belonged to Joash the Abiezrite, where his son Gideon was threshing wheat in a winepress to keep it from the Midianites. When the angel of the LORD appeared to Gideon, he said "The LORD is with you, mighty warrior."
>
> "But sir," Gideon replied, "if the Lord is with us, why has all this happened to us?
>
> Where are all his wonders that our fathers told us about when they said, 'Did not the LORD bring us up out of

Egypt?' But now the LORD has abandoned us and put us into the hand of Midian."

The LORD turned to him and said, "Go in the strength you have and save Israel out of Midian's hand. Am I not sending you?"

"But LORD," Gideon asked, "how can I save Israel? My clan is the weakest in Manasseh, and I am the least in my family."

The LORD answered, "I will be with you, and you will strike down the Midianites as if there were but one man." (Judges 6:11-16)

Wheat was normally threshed in an open space, allowing air to blow away the chaff. Since Gideon was performing this task in a winepress, which was often a pit below ground, he was likely hiding from the Midianites. Therefore, imagine Gideon's startled response when referred to as a "mighty warrior." These words surely felt mocking to one who wasn't acting like a warrior. But if this initial greeting seemed out of character, consider how the next words sounded: "Go in the strength you have and save Israel." In other words, God was instructing Gideon to conquer the very people he was hiding from. Whenever I read this passage, I think of the former TV show, *Candid Camera*, which caught people in embarrassing moments. Had Gideon lived during its existence, he would probably have looked around to see who was playing a trick on him.

To be fair, it's hard to know how we would handle an encounter like this with God—but Gideon's response was completely uninspiring. First, he questioned God about the disconnect between His previous care and current abandonment (conveniently ignoring his nation's disobedience). Next, Gideon insisted that he couldn't possibly do what God asked. Noting his inferior social status, Gideon questioned how God could possibly expect him to lead others. His protests echoed Moses' response when asked to lead Israel out of Egypt—and were equally ineffective in relieving Gideon of this assignment.

God asked Gideon to do something incredibly challenging—but notice how **He gently led Gideon from where he was into what he could be.** This was not an uncaring shove by our Lord, but a gradual progression that enabled Gideon to grow in confidence and self-understanding. And it reveals how lovingly and personally God facilitates our journey of growth. First, the Lord agreed to Gideon's request for a sign to confirm that this assignment really was from Him. Gideon later requested another sign—and then another! Though the Lord anointed and used many judges, Gideon was the only one recorded who required these reassuring signs. Biblical scholar J.C. Exum observed, "No character in the book receives more divine assurance than Gideon, and none displays more doubt."

God also prepared Gideon for his big assignment with a smaller initial one. Replacing his father's altar to Baal with one to the Lord risked upsetting Gideon's father and others in his community—but that was an easier next step than leading an army into battle. Once again, we see Gideon's lack of confidence: "Because he was afraid of his family and the men of the town, he did it at night rather than in the daytime" (Judges 6:27). When angry town leaders demanded consequences for Gideon's actions, his father surprisingly stood up for his son. God knew what Gideon was capable of and met him there. After Gideon faithfully accomplished this task, the Lord entrusted him with the larger assignment of conquering the Midianites. This led to Gideon's greatest test of faith yet.

Gideon convinced 32,000 to follow him into battle against the Midianites. Though that's an impressive number, his army was only a quarter the size of the enemy's—and then Gideon's challenge became greater. To make obvious the Lord's role in victory, He whittled Gideon's army down to less than one percent of its original number:

> The LORD said to Gideon, "You have too many men. I cannot deliver Midian into their hands, or Israel would boast against me, 'My own strength has saved me.' Now announce to the army, 'Anyone who trembles with fear may turn back and leave Mount Gilead.'" So twenty-two thousand men left, while ten thousand remained.
>
> But the LORD said to Gideon, "There are still too many men. Take them down to the water, and I will thin them out for you there. If I say, 'This one shall go with you,' he shall go; but if I say, 'This one shall not go with you,' he shall not go."
>
> So Gideon took the men down to the water. There the LORD told him, "Separate those who lap the water with their tongues as a dog laps from those who kneel down to drink." Three hundred of them drank from cupped hands, lapping like dogs. All the rest got down on their knees to drink.
>
> The LORD said to Gideon, "With the three hundred men that lapped I will save you and give the Midianites into your hands. Let all the others go home." (Judges 7:2-7)

Imagine being defended by an attorney who had 100 witnesses on your behalf but only chose to use one. Or flying with a pilot who announced that she wouldn't use most of her flight instruments. How would it feel to go into surgery with a doctor who sent most of his surgical team out of the operating room? Think how loudly you'd protest—then understand how Gideon must have felt. His willingness to lead 300 into battle against 137,000 reveals how far he'd come. Yet God still encouraged him one more time.

Before Gideon's battle with the Midianites, a tender initiative by God occurred. The Lord said to Gideon, "If you are afraid to attack . . ." (Judges 7:10). Of course, Gideon was afraid to attack! His hesitation was obvious throughout this story, his army was reduced to 300, and he had plenty of reasons to fear the battle ahead. Rather than be disgusted by Gideon's continued uncertainty, God acknowledged what he was feeling. The Lord encouraged Gideon with a suggestion that bolstered his confidence and led to triumph in battle. God wanted to deliver not only the Israelites from their oppressors, but also Gideon from his fear. Gideon's success against the Midianites revealed that he really did have more going for him than he'd realized. And it invites us to consider if the same might be true of us.

Our Story

Two surprising events occurred near the end of my junior year in college. First, my dorm's Resident Director encouraged me to apply to be Resident Advisor of a dorm floor the following year. I had never considered myself a leader, nor had any ever referred to me as one. However, prompted by that encouragement, I applied, was offered a position, and was subsequently assigned one of the most challenging floors on campus. Weeks later, the outgoing leadership of a male student organization I was a member of requested permission to nominate me president for the next year. Again, I was stunned. I agreed, was elected—and prepared for two leadership roles that I hadn't seen coming. In both instances, others saw potential in me that I didn't know was there.

Gideon's story reveals God's ability to do the same for us. His initial salutation of "mighty warrior" revealed potential that was a complete surprise to Gideon. God's instruction to "go in the strength you have" indicated that Gideon already possessed all he needed for this assignment, which was news to Gideon. Throughout the Bible, God didn't select those jumping up and down shouting, "Pick me!" **He usually chose individuals like Gideon, who were surprised to learn the Lord saw more in them than they did.** As a result, a fugitive in the desert (Moses) led God's people into the Promised Land, a farmer chasing after a donkey (Saul) became Israel's first king, and a young shepherd overlooked within his own family (David) became its second. God expanded their self-understanding of what they could do, and He longs to do the same with us. Author Eugene Peterson explained, **"There is an enormous gap between what we think we can do and what God calls us to do. Our ideas of what we can do or want to do are trivial; God's ideas for us are grand."**

This story assures us that God understands any feelings of uncertainty or vulnerability when facing new challenges. As the Lord invites us into new opportunities, He'll meet us in our insecurity like He did with Gideon. But God won't stop nudging us toward what He knows we can do. If we're inclined to remain within already familiar experiences, two actions can help us more fully live out what the Lord has placed within us.

1. Listen for God's Insights
I've forgotten much of what I learned in college, but the JoHari

Window is one concept I do remember. Briefly, the JoHari Window consists of four quadrants that represent knowledge about us. The left two quadrants reflect our self-knowledge, and the right two what's not known to us. The top two quadrants signify information others have about us, and the bottom two what's not publicly known about us. Taken together, the upper left quadrant represents what I know about myself that others also know: for example, the color of my hair. The lower left quadrant represents what I know about myself that others don't know: perhaps some deep fear, or an embarrassing moment from my past. The upper right quadrant represents what others know about me that I don't know about myself: that awkward spinach in my teeth that everyone but me can see. Finally, the lower right quadrant represents what neither I nor others know about me: insights yet to be learned. This model offers a helpful illustration of how much there still is to learn about ourselves, that God already knows.

JoHari Window

	Known to Self	Not Known to Self
Known to Others	Open	Blind
Not Known to Others	Hidden	Unknown

A group calling themselves the *Barbie Liberation Organization* purchased hundreds of Barbie and GI Joe dolls in 1993. After switching the voice boxes between them, group members snuck the dolls back onto store shelves. Imagine the trauma of children who heard their Barbie doll exclaim in a deep voice, "*Vengeance is mine!*" Or those who heard their GI Joe doll say with a high-pitch, "*The beach is the place for summer!*" What existed within was radically different from what outer appearances suggested. **Our Creator intimately understands what He's planted deep within us, even if some things aren't yet obvious to us or to others.** No matter how far along we are in life, there's potential, giftedness, or areas of deep passion that we've yet to discover.

This makes life a progressive journey of learning more about ourselves than we've previously understood. We've discovered much by now: what we most desire, what moves us to act, and what fears tend to hold us back. Yet the JoHari Window illustrates that our self-understanding is still incomplete. Fortunately, we have a God who delights in revealing to us what we've yet to learn about ourselves. But it's incumbent upon us to intentionally and persistently ask the Lord to share His understanding about us. As we pursue and are receptive to the insights God reveals, our self-awareness of what we can do will increase.

How will you allow God to enlarge your self-understanding?

2. Move to the Deeper End

I took summer swimming lessons at our city pool during my childhood. Over a few summers I advanced from the shallow end of the large pool where my feet could touch bottom, to the other end of the pool that seemed a mile deep (actually, probably 10 feet). That pool comes to mind when I read Gideon's story. Many of us prefer to linger in the shallow end of life, where our feet can touch bottom; it feels safer than the deep end, where risks and discomfort are greater. But the uncomfortable truth is that **God tends to reside in the deep end of life, and He beckons us to move from our preferred shallow end to where He is.** Our Lord's inclination is to move us, like Gideon, outside our comfort zone. He does this to enlarge our capacity, deepen our faith, and share with the world what He's placed within us. Though this can be life-giving, many of us would rather remain within where things are convenient and familiar.

Gideon's initial responses reveal his preference to remain where he was, rather than accept God's risky invitation to join Him where the water was deeper. Sure enough, when Gideon emerged from the winepress, life became more challenging. Yet when Gideon later looked back over his life, I doubt he regretted responding to God's summons to the deeper end, for it led to a much bigger life. Gideon learned more about himself and about his God, and he accomplished more than he ever thought possible.

Yes, our Lord's invitations into new places can prompt fear: fear that there won't be enough of us for what He asks; fear that mistakes or failure will result in falling short; or perhaps most commonly, fear that we won't like where God takes us. But we rarely find God giving out easy assignments in the Bible. In His wisdom, He knows comfort comes at the expense of using less of what He's given us. God also never invites us into something new by ourselves; He'll always accompany us into it. This understanding undergirds pastor Ken Brumley's three truths about God's will for our lives: *it will be about others; it will often be beyond our resources; and because of that, it will always be an opportunity to experience more of God.* Gideon's story reveals the Lord's desire that we use more of ourselves than we're sometimes willing to settle for. If God asked this of Gideon, is there any reason to think He won't do the same with us?

An early Church Father named Irenaeus declared, "**The glory of God is a fully alive human being.**" We become more fully alive when we allow our Lord to grow and stretch us through His invitations into new opportunities. That's why Henry Blackaby encouraged in *Experiencing God*, "find out where God is and join Him there." The Lord has already used us in different ways throughout our years. Allow Gideon's story to introduce the possibility of new opportunities still before you in the deep end of life.

What's one way you could move toward the deeper end of the pool (life) with God?

Final Thought

It's natural to assume that the mold of who we are has been firmly set by our later years. We're grateful for how God has already transformed us, but suspect there's little new left for Him to do. However, that's contrary to Paul's declaration that God "who began a good work in you will carry it on to completion until the day of Christ Jesus" (Philippians 1:6). Notice when the Lord's work in us will cease (hint: it isn't when we turn 70, 90, or even 100). As we seek to finish well, these words provide encouragement that God isn't finished creating new beauty within us.

I saw a beautiful example of this in Italy a few years ago. While in Florence, I visited the Accademia Gallery to see Michelangelo's statue of David. That work of art was even more magnificent than I'd anticipated—but my attention was captured that day by another display. Along a hallway before reaching David were a series of partially completed statues known as the Prisoners. Michelangelo began carving each of these statues out of blocks of marble during his career, but never completed them. Today, visitors can see figures of great beauty emerging from the stone still containing them.

When I left the Accademia that day, the picture I purchased wasn't of David, but of one of these Prisoners—and it sits in my office where I can see it each day. I've found these sculptures a powerful reminder of God's chiseling us out of the stone of life; regardless of beauty that He's already brought forth, there's still more creative work to come. God isn't done creating new definition of who we are from the material of our lives. There's still much that He longs to reveal to us about who we are and what we're capable of in our remaining years.

Don't assume God's transforming work in you is nearly complete or that you fully understand your potential by now. We move toward finishing well by inviting the Lord to show us where He wants to mold and shape new facets of beauty and remaining responsive to His work. This will also help us better accept the next chapter's exploration of the incredible value within each of us.

Chapter 6

UNDERSTAND YOUR GREAT VALUE

"We put our labels on people the way designers sew labels on their clothes. And then we let the labels tell us what people are and what they are worth."

— Lewis Smedes

In *My Creator, My Friend*, Bruce Larson wrote of a wealthy nineteenth-century farmer named Worthy Taylor who hired a young man to help one summer. Jim faithfully completed his chores each day, slept in the barn, and ate his meals with the family. He also fell in love with Taylor's daughter during those summer months. But Jim's request to marry her was rebuffed by Taylor, who noted that the young man had no means to support a family and seemingly little future.

At the end of the summer, Jim moved on from the farm. Taylor became even more prosperous over the next thirty-five years, and eventually decided to tear down his old barn and build a bigger one. When he did, Taylor discovered Jim's full name carved in the rafter over the hayloft where he had slept: "James A Garfield"—by then the 20th President of the United States.

We make assumptions about others that impact how we value and interact with them—and they do the same with us. If these perceptions remain unchallenged by subsequent interactions, they harden over time and become our perceived truth about a person.

It's not uncommon to feel unfairly characterized by someone's inaccurate initial assumptions; breaking out of that box and reshaping another's perception of us is never easy. Unfortunately, assumptions tend to possess an undervaluing nature; they limit rather than empower. Author Brennan Manning explained the damage they can do: "Most of the time we're wrong in our judgments about others. The tragedy is that our attention centers on what people are not, rather than on what they are and who they might become."

Society's assumptions of older generations too often diminish the value that others see and influence their interactions. As our pace becomes more deliberate and unhurried, some perceive only that we're in the way, slowing them down. When Deborah and I moved to Florida years ago for my first ordained position, the most frequent comment I heard about older residents was that their driving slowed traffic for everyone else (years later, I'm beginning to resemble that remark). Additionally, a younger generation's high value on productivity and accomplishment too often discounts the wisdom and experience that older generations still have to offer. Sometimes, older adults aren't given much consideration at all; we're simply overlooked and undervalued by those around us.

In what circumstances are you most likely to feel overlooked or undervalued by others?

Finishing well involves feeling good about ourselves, and the value that our presence in this world still provides. We refuse to accept less than positive stereotypes of older generations; instead, we eagerly embrace all that we still have going for us. This approach doesn't come easily, though, for it pushes against a common assumption that older adults are simply living out their remaining years. Our next story is of a man perceived negatively by others— and it sounds like he worked hard to deserve it. But while the crowd around Zacchaeus had written him off, we see the life-giving difference that Jesus' love and acceptance made in his life and can have in ours.

Zacchaeus' Story

The IRS tends to be poorly thought of among the American population. Now imagine your perception of this tax collection agency if: 1) you were provided no annual tax table explaining how much you owed; 2) you had to take a tax collector's word for your payment; and 3) that person was a neighbor, whose wealth steadily increased. That describes the tax system during Jesus' time. Rome sold to the highest bidder the right to collect taxes, then communicated what it expected to receive. Tax collectors profited by adding their cut—and because they were backed by Rome, people had no choice but to pay. If a person couldn't do so, tax collectors offered to loan the amount due at a high interest rate.

This was a lucrative business, and Jericho was one of Palestine's greatest tax centers when Jesus visited. Because it was on a major trade route to Jerusalem, just 15 miles away, caravans regularly passed through Jericho. The area's fertile agriculture also created wealthy plantations. Illustrating this city's riches, Marc Antony is said to have once given Jericho to Cleopatra, with Arabia thrown in.

One of Jericho's tax collectors was a man named Zacchaeus. He was wealthy, which means he did his job well; however, this resulted in few friends outside the community of tax collectors. Zacchaeus was considered a traitor because he worked for Rome, and an extortionist because he became rich at the expense of fellow citizens. Public perception of Zacchaeus and other tax collectors was so low, they were barred from worshiping in the synagogue. Tax collectors were lumped socially in the same category as thieves and murderers.

Frederick Buechner described Zacchaeus as "a sawed off little social disaster with a big bank account and a crooked job." But when Jesus affirmed his value, something changed within Zacchaeus:

> Jesus entered Jericho and was passing through. A man was there by the name of Zacchaeus; he was a chief tax collector and was wealthy. He wanted to see who Jesus was, but being a short man he could not, because of the crowd. So he ran ahead and climbed a sycamore-fig tree to see him, since Jesus was coming that way.
>
> When Jesus reached the spot, he looked up and said to him, "Zacchaeus, come down immediately. I must stay at your house today." So he came down at once and welcomed him gladly.
>
> All the people saw this and began to mutter, "He has gone to be the guest of a sinner."
>
> But Zacchaeus stood up and said to the Lord, "Look Lord! Here and now I give half of my possessions to the poor, and if I have cheated anybody out of anything, I will pay back four times the amount."
>
> Jesus said to him, "Today salvation has come to this house, because this man, too, is a son of Abraham. For the Son of Man came to seek and to save what was lost." (Luke 19:1-10)

The Greek word describing Zacchaeus' desire to see Jesus implies continual effort and suggests an eagerness to watch Him pass. We don't know whether Zacchaeus' actions were prompted by curiosity, or perhaps by Jesus' reputation as a friend of all. We do know that it created a dilemma for Zacchaeus. Because he was short, he couldn't see over those who lined the road—and Zacchaeus' social standing added to the challenge. Commenting on this passage, William

Barclay explained: "To mingle in this crowd was dangerous, for many would seek the opportunity to get back with a nudge, push, or a kick." So, Zacchaeus climbed a tree. This elevated him above those who were taller and provided safety from the crowd. But it wasn't among the more dignified positions along Jesus' route, which may be why this detail was included.

The crowd that welcomed Jesus likely included a number of respectable people who were community leaders or had devoted their lives to serving God and others. Many would surely have been happy to host this famous visitor. But Jesus seemingly had eyes only for this tax collector in a tree, and He invited Himself to Zacchaeus' home. Brennan Manning noted that in Eastern society, sharing a meal with someone was a symbol of trust and forgiveness. Thus, this dinner connection conveyed Jesus' desire to enter a relationship with Zacchaeus—which Luke tells us seemed to "all the people" like a waste of Jesus' time. They cautioned their celebrity visitor: "Um, Jesus—he's not the kind of person you want to be associated with." All anyone could see about Zacchaeus was his label of "sinner."

I'll never forget the response of a homeless person years ago when I told him that Jesus loved him; his face caked with dirt, he looked me in the eye and replied, "I really don't know why He would." Sadly, his self-understanding was undoubtedly shaped by years of others' devaluing assumptions about and treatment of him. Similarly, Zacchaeus' sense of value couldn't help but be influenced by the comments and social exclusion that he experienced.

In a shocking moment, Jesus affirmed that this tax collector had as much value as anyone else in the crowd. His actions offered Zacchaeus a welcome contrast to others' value-reducing perceptions. Jesus stated at the story's conclusion, "The Son of Man has come to seek and to save what is lost" (Luke 19:10). At the core of this assurance, Jesus gave His life on the cross to defeat sin's power to separate us from God. By initiating a relationship with Zacchaeus, Jesus also revealed a desire to save him—and us—from others' devaluing and life-shaping perceptions. He longs to restore our dignity and help us understand our tremendous value, especially when it's unacknowledged by the crowd around us. Jesus' surprising initiative led to an equally surprising reaction from Zacchaeus, who offered to repay those whom he'd cheated. His response illustrates the life-changing impact of feeling valued.

Our Story

I worked on my college campus the summer after I graduated; for a few of those weeks I helped a carpenter renovate an executive office near the school President's office. I can still remember my interaction with the President's secretary—or rather, lack of interaction. Whenever I walked by the office, she glanced up, saw me in my work clothes, then quickly looked down again without acknowledgement. It was obvious that she didn't think I belonged there; I was a temporary intrusion into her world.

After a week, I grew tired of this devaluing treatment—so I entered her office one day and asked to see the President! I went on to explain that I wanted to talk about my senior honors project, which he and I had previously discussed. Her blank facial expression upon hearing my request is probably the only reason I still remember that encounter. It was obvious that the assumption she'd formed of me made it hard to know how to respond. I fully enjoyed that moment—but it was a sad reminder how easily others' perceptions and actions can devalue us.

Inaccurate assumptions by the crowd around us aren't the only cause of feeling overlooked and undervalued. Our own self-assessment of the value we have to offer can also be influenced by unhealthy and inaccurate measurements. Robert McGee addressed this in his book, *Search for Significance*, suggesting that our self-perception is too often shaped by the equation, *Self-worth = Performance + Others' Opinions.*

After reading this book years ago, I shared McGee's equation with a class I was teaching and asked, "How many of you believe this is true?" One individual in the back of the room raised her hand—then quickly lowered it after realizing she was the only one. I remember thinking at the time that hers may have been the only honest response. Warning bells instinctively go off when we hear an equation like this; it just doesn't sound right. Yet we're still inclined to evaluate our significance to the world around us by these elements.

Soren Kierkegaard wrote a parable of a store that was broken into one night. The burglars didn't steal anything, but instead switched the price tags on all the items. Inexpensive items suddenly cost a fortune, and expensive items became a bargain. In this parable, no one noticed the mis-valuing of these items when the store opened the next morning. Kierkegaard's conclusion offered a sobering reflection on our capacity to mis-perceive value: "The people of my day have no ability to tell the truly valuable from the truly worthless."

Both elements in McGee's equation can falsely shape our perceived worth. Performance may have influenced a sense of value during younger years when we were establishing ourselves. In later years, it tends to diminish in importance. But other's opinions of us continue to strongly influence our feelings of significance at any age. For this reason, let's explore two approaches that can help us maintain a healthy understanding of what we have to offer.

1. Choose Wisely Among the Voices

Over our lifetime, people reflect back to us their perception of our value. During our early years, value was conveyed by our parents—hopefully high value, but that's unfortunately not always a given. At school, our value was affirmed in friendships that we developed; it may also have been chipped away through other students' hostile words or actions. Value was reinforced in later years by friends or a spouse who shared life with us. Without realizing it, our self-perceived value is often shaped by what others reflect back to us. If we're not careful, we end up placing our sense of worth in their hands.

Adding to the challenge is advertising that insists a product will positively influence others' opinions of us. I saw a blatant example of this years ago in a television commercial by a car company I won't name (it rhymes with Texas). The ad contained no spoken words—just four phrases appearing on the screen, one after another:

You're at a stoplight . . .
It will last 20 seconds . . .
This may be the only time someone sees you . . .
How do you want to be remembered?

There was no mention of car performance or affordability; the pitch was simply that others would think well of a person in this car.

We also tend to prioritize which voices matter most to us. A seminary professor, Archibald Hart, noted that we create a mental grandstand of people whose opinions about us we most value. Some voices of approval are so important, they can continue influencing us even after a person's death. Unfortunately, Hart observed that we often long most for approval from individuals whose "well done" has been challenging to earn: perhaps a demanding parent, an unforgiving boss, or a former spouse. This concept rang true when I heard it and assessed who I most longed to hear affirmation from in my mental grandstand.

Age and wisdom enable us to filter out negative or unhelpful feedback about our worth more easily than when we were younger. But not always. Therefore, it's important to identify which opinions matter most and best reflect who we really are. We want to allow these voices to shape how we feel about ourselves, and minimize the influence of other, less helpful opinions. On the flip side, we have opportunities to affirm others with our validating and encouraging input.

Whose approval tends to be most important to you at this time in life?

2. Listen for God's Opinion

After exploring the unhealthiness of performance and opinions in shaping our self-perception, McGee suggested a more helpful equation: *Self Worth = God's Truth About You*. But what is God's truth? Perhaps Max Lucado put it best when he wrote, "In the eyes of the King, you have value simply because you are." The significance of this, as Zacchaeus discovered, is that God's love for us is constant; this unchanging source of value provides an encouraging counter-balance to the headwinds of indifference or disapproval by the crowd around us. Noting that God's love is fueled not by our goodness but by His grace, pastor Mike Platter remarked, **"God has forever taken the thermostat of His love for you out of your hands."**

Former Olympic diving great Greg Louganis was once asked how he handled the stress of international competition. Louganis responded that his final thought after climbing to the top of the diving platform was, "Even if I blow this dive, my mother will still love me." God's love and acceptance provides a stabilizing opinion in our lives the same way a mother's love provided reassuring grounding for this diver. Yes, the Lord will always seek to move us beyond where we've settled, as Christ did with Zacchaeus. But these holy nudges flow out of grace and acceptance, rather than a "not good enough" opinion of us.

When Jackie Kennedy Onassis' estate was auctioned in 1996, a worn footstool sold for over $33,000, and a silver tape measure for nearly $49,000. The highest bid of more than $500,000 was for a walnut tobacco humidor that had belonged to President Kennedy. These common items are normally unworthy of such lofty prices, but were valued so highly because of who they belonged to. Our value ultimately has nothing to do with the ebb and flow of what others think of us. Instead, it's grounded in the unchanging opinion of our Creator, to whom we each belong. Julian of Norwich described the difference this can make, writing, **"The greatest honor we can give to God is to live gladly because of the knowledge of his love."**

Zacchaeus' story reveals a contrast between the crowd that had written him off, and Jesus who lovingly accepted him. Our Lord reinforced Zacchaeus' value that day in Jericho and wants to do the same for us. The next time you're tempted to feel overlooked or undervalued because of other's assumptions or treatment, remember the unchanging value that you have to God. The better we learn to allow His opinion to shape our sense of significance, the more confidently we'll lean forward into finishing well.

"In the eyes of the King, you have value simply because you are." What helps you believe this truth?

Final Thought

Mary Ann Bird described in the third-person a formative childhood experience that countered voices from the crowd and reinforced her sense of value:

Mary Ann was born with a cleft palate before the time when reparative surgery was easily available. She was also deaf in one ear. In school, her classmates teased her without mercy. She couldn't blow up a balloon without holding her nose or drink from a water fountain successfully.

"Oh Mary Ann," her classmates would say, "What happened to your lip?"

"I cut it on a piece of glass," she would lie.

One of the worst experiences at school, she reported, was the day of the annual hearing test. The teacher would call each child to her desk, and the child would cover first one ear, and then the other. The teacher would whisper something to the child like "The sky is blue" or "You have new shoes." This was "the whisper test." If the teacher's phrase was heard and repeated, the child passed the test. To avoid the humiliation of failure, Mary Ann would always cheat on the test, secretly cupping her hand over her one good ear so that she could still hear what the teacher said.

One year Mary Ann was in the class of Miss Leonard, one of the most beloved teachers in the school. Every student, including Mary Ann, wanted to be noticed by her.

Then came the day of the dreaded hearing test. When her turn came, Mary Ann was called to the teacher's desk. As Mary Ann cupped her hand over her good ear, Miss Leonard leaned forward to whisper. "I waited for those words," Mary Ann wrote, "which God must have put into her mouth, those seven words which changed my life."

Miss Leonard did not say, "The sky is blue" or "You have new shoes." No, Miss Leonard carefully leaned over to get as close as possible and whispered, "I wish you were my little girl."

Every day, God whispers to us affirming messages of our value. Allow His voice to rise above others in shaping your self-understanding. And look for ways to be the Lord's encouraging voice to others.

Chapter 7

CULTIVATE A SPIRIT OF GRATITUDE

"You are alive! Celebrate accordingly."

— Subject line of an email advertisement

A mother and son were suddenly surprised by a tornado one day. The mother grabbed a tree with one hand and her son with the other and held tightly onto both—but the wind was too strong, and the boy was eventually pulled into the air. The woman cried out to God, promising that if He returned her son, she'd be grateful to Him for the rest of her life.

Suddenly the boy fell gently from the sky, landing in a large branch above her; he was wind-blown, but safe. The mother joyfully helped him the rest of the way down. But then, after examining her son, she looked up and complained, "Lord, he had a hat!"

Gratitude is an essential quality for finishing well. Dwelling upon the good in our lives fuels a buoyancy of spirit and helps balance our perspective of what's not good. And let's face it: gratitude makes us more fun to be around. Psychologist Derrick Carpenter highlighted some of gratitude's benefits: "People who regularly practice gratitude . . . experience more positive emotions, feel more alive, sleep better, express more compassion and kindness, and even have stronger immune systems." Gordon Macdonald declared in *The Life God Blesses*, **"The quality of gratitude is at the center of a healthy soul."**

One chapter in McDonald's book is intriguingly titled, *What Kind of An Old Man Do You Want to Be?* Seeking to answer this question for himself, MacDonald identified older men whom he admired, and characteristics in their lives that he wanted to imitate. Gratitude is mentioned first, but MacDonald noted, ". . . gratitude appears to take a licking in the aging process. It is replaced by a sense of entitlement, of grudging demands. In contrast, the spirit of thankfulness does not come naturally. It must be worked at as a discipline for most of us." This may be due in part to losses that come with age; gratitude can be more difficult when it feels like experiences and abilities are being subtracted from our lives, rather than new ones added. Our spirit within can also harden with time, as characteristics during younger years become more entrenched later in life. If we perceived in previous decades that what we had was lacking, that mindset becomes more prevalent in later years.

Gratitude acknowledges that we have much good to celebrate at any age. In our next story, a woman beautifully models this quality. While we don't know her name, Luke was compelled to include her response to Jesus in his Gospel because it was so remarkable.

A Woman's Story

This book emerged from my interest in exploring biblical stories. I enjoy fleshing out details that might be overlooked and identifying points of connection with our lives today. This unnamed woman's story presents a challenge because we're told so little about her. Most scholars believe she was a prostitute, based on Luke's description that she "lived a sinful life" (Luke 7:37). Some believe that she's Mary, the sister of Lazarus, based on similar stories in the other Gospels that mention Mary by name. I do not. For one thing, Matthew, Mark and John place their accounts in Bethany, where Lazarus lived. However, Luke's story occurred in the northern part of the country, based on references to Jesus' ministry in Nain and Capernaum. Additionally, Jesus' focus upon hospitality and forgiveness of sins in Luke's story differs from the other accounts. Beyond these glimpses, our only information about this woman comes from her story:

> When one of the Pharisees invited Jesus to have dinner with him, he went to the Pharisee's house and reclined at the table. A woman in that town who lived a sinful life learned that Jesus was eating at the Pharisee's house, so she came there with an alabaster jar of perfume. As she stood behind him at his feet weeping, she began to wet his feet with her tears. Then she wiped them with her hair, kissed them and poured perfume on them.
>
> When the Pharisee who had invited him saw this, he said to himself, "If this man were a prophet, he would know who is touching him and what kind of woman she is—that she is a sinner."
>
> Jesus answered him, "Simon, I have something to tell you."
>
> "Tell me, teacher," he said.
>
> "Two people owed money to a certain moneylender. One owed him five hundred denarii, and the other fifty. Neither of them had the money to pay him back, so he forgave the debts of both. Now which of them will love him more?"
>
> Simon replied, "I suppose the one who had the bigger debt forgiven."
>
> "You have judged correctly," Jesus said.
>
> Then he turned toward the woman and said to Simon, "Do

you see this woman? I came into your house. You did not give me any water for my feet, but she wet my feet with her tears and wiped them with her hair. You did not give me a kiss, but this woman, from the time I entered, has not stopped kissing my feet. You did not put oil on my head, but she has poured perfume on my feet. Therefore, I tell you, her many sins have been forgiven—as her great love has shown. But whoever has been forgiven little, loves little."

Then Jesus said to her, "Your sins are forgiven."

The other guests began to say among themselves, "Who is this who even forgives sins?"

Jesus said to the woman, "Your faith has saved you; go in peace." (Luke 7:36-50)

This woman's actions were socially inappropriate on multiple levels. Though the public was often allowed to watch gatherings like this from the edge of the room, she wasn't supposed to leave the sideline and enter the field of play among dinner guests. It was also inappropriate for women to approach men in public. Adding to the awkwardness, no decent woman ever let down her hair in public, as this woman did to wipe Jesus' feet. The underlying scandal, of course, was that her reputation was far from decent.

This woman's actions suggest that Jesus had significantly impacted her in some way. For one thing, the perfume she poured on his feet was probably expensive. Then there was the personal price she paid for attending this gathering. Anyone with a reputation as bad as hers probably went out of their way to avoid additional ridicule or rejection by remaining inconspicuous. Yet she entered the home of a Pharisee who she knew thought poorly of her; she also understood that her actions would invite additional criticism and attention.

Despite all these factors, she was compelled to act as she did.

Anticipating Simon's critical response, Jesus told a parable of two men in debt; one owed an estimated 20 month's wages, and the other approximately two month's wages. The forgiveness of both debts would have surprised Jesus' listeners, for this practice could put a money lender out of business. Simon grudgingly answered Jesus' concluding question by acknowledging that the one experiencing the greatest forgiveness presumably felt the greatest love and gratitude.

Because Pharisees sought to avoid offending God in any way, the perceived need for forgiveness was small and subsequent reasons for gratitude few. Their hard work to maintain godly lifestyles left less to give God credit for. Jesus understood how this prevented Simon from living out this woman's thankful response. So, His parable gently summarized the Gospel message: God generously extends grace, and our response becomes grateful acknowledgement of what He's done. Jesus encouraged Simon to learn from this unnamed woman's example—as can we.

Our Story

One of my favorite stories is of a physically handicapped sales-man selling magazines in a neighborhood. A resident noticed him working his way down the street, laboring to walk. Eventually arriving at this person's home, the salesman navigated the front steps, rang the doorbell, and asked if the resident would like to make a purchase. A conversation ensued, and the homeowner eventually asked if this was a difficult job. The salesman replied that it was. When the homeowner asked how he felt about that, the salesman's response was surprisingly positive. Before he could catch himself, the homeowner blurted out, "But you're handicapped. Doesn't that color your world?"

The salesman replied, "Yes, it does. But I get to choose the color."

Gratitude is a choice, and its presence or absence dramatically impacts our perspective on life. When our children were growing up, we taught them to say, "Thank you." Those words are easily learned, but genuine gratitude deep within can be harder to cultivate. For one thing, we too often take for granted the good in our lives. John Ortberg noted, "The default mode of the sinful human race is entitlement, the belief that this gift or that experience that God placed in my path is rightfully mine. I am owed . . . The more you think you're entitled to, the less you will be grateful for."

Gratitude is also dampened by preoccupation with what we don't have. Mark Twain wrote of this inclination, "You don't know quite what it is you do want, but it just fairly makes your heart ache you want it so." This preoccupation is fueled in multiple ways. Advertisers insist that we're missing out if we don't have their product. Losses and disappointment along the way can fuel this perception. Additionally, the good that we experience may be overshadowed by what we see others enjoying. Consider this description, years ago, of an evening with actor Paul Newman:

> "A couple weeks ago, we went out to have dinner with him in Connecticut, and we're driving home and I'm thinking to myself: Here's Paul. What is he? Sixty? Sixty-one? He looks great, feels great, has a lot of money, gives to great causes, he's in love with his wife, he races his cars when he wants to, makes a movie when he wants to, he's incredibly happy and still has that face that looks the way it did when he was twenty. By the time we got home, I wanted to shoot myself."

The speaker was Robert Redford.

Brennan Manning suggested, **"Gratitude arises from the lived perception . . . of all of life as grace—as an undeserved and unearned gift from the Father's hand."** We contribute to this perception when we replace expectations of what we should have or a focus upon what we don't have with a grateful posture for all that the Lord provides. Three actions can help us develop and maintain this posture of gratitude.

1. Notice

Before Deborah and I recently moved across town, my morning walks began with a beautiful view of Pikes Peak looming before me. I wish I could tell you it inspired me each day—but to be honest, I was usually so deep in thought, I didn't even notice it. Preoccupation with each day's demands diminishes our capacity to notice blessings. Author Ken Gire lamented: "It's a great loss that we awake to so many gifts on a given day, not only without opening them, but without knowing they are even there for us to open."

Intentionally noticing our gifts creates a helpful counterbalance to our inclination to focus upon what's not good. Suggestions from visitors at Bridger Wilderness Park in Wyoming humorously illustrate this tendency:

- Trails need to be reconstructed. Please avoid building trails that go uphill.
- Too many bugs and leeches and spiders and spider webs. Please spray the wilderness to rid the area of these pests.
- The coyotes made too much noise last night and kept me awake. Please eradicate these annoying animals.
- Escalators would help on steep sections.
- Too many rocks in the mountains.

What captured the attention of these visitors wasn't the beauty around them, but what they didn't like.

One woman beautifully modelled this act of noticing when she said of her life, "So much has been given to me, I have no time to ponder over that which has been denied." Remarkably, it was Helen Keller who said this. Though illness at the age of two left her without sight or hearing, Keller didn't allow what she lacked to define her life; she looked for blessings to celebrate. Keller's outlook reminds us that even when life isn't as we desire, there's still good to acknowledge. We have eyes to read these words, a heart faithfully pumping, air to breathe, and many other blessings. How many other good gifts can we identify each day?

The woman anointing Jesus' feet still had a poor reputation that limited others' perceptions of her. Any life change she felt compelled to make wouldn't be easy. But her actions revealed a focus upon the good that Jesus seems to have introduced in her life. Thornton Wilder noted, **"We can only be said to be alive in those moments when our hearts are conscious of our treasures."** Like the woman in our story, we choose the color of gratitude by noticing and naming our treasures. My wife Deborah did just that during this year's Lenten season. She decided to record and daily add to a list of reasons for gratitude; six weeks later, her list contained more than 450 blessings.

What reasons for gratitude do you have today?

2. Remember
Noticing reasons for gratitude prompts us to look around us; remembering occurs when we look behind us. Reflecting upon blessings from our past can shape our present perspective in deeply meaningful ways. Remembering and celebrating blessings previously experi-

enced also multiplies our moments of gratitude. Here's a silly example: I've been a season ticket holder for the Colorado Avalanche National Hockey League team for 13 years—and they've been very lean years. This year the team made the playoffs in consecutive seasons for the first time during this period. Though they qualified a week before I'm writing this, I experience a repeated sense of delight each time I remember this accomplishment. Gratitude about previous good that we've experienced works the same way. Obviously, a memory's good feelings wear off at some point; that's why it's important to regularly replenish our memories with fresh reasons for gratitude.

Ignatius of Loyola wrote that "ingratitude is the most abominable of sins . . . For it is a forgetting of the graces, benefits and blessings received." The word "*remember*" occurs more than 200 times throughout the Bible. God repeatedly instructed the Israelites throughout the Old Testament to remember what He'd done for them. Their frequent forgetting resulted in grumbling rather than gratitude. But remembering isn't only a problem for the Israelites. Our memories are also fickle: we recall a high school memory, or where we were during the first moon landing. But we forget something God did for us a month or even a week ago.

What's one thing from your past for which you're grateful?

We don't know when Jesus first crossed paths with this woman in our story, but her memory of His impact fueled gratitude and compelled her to act—leading to our third action.

3. Express

A Hasidic parable tells of two poor farmers who met their rabbi on the road during difficult times. When he asked how they were, the first farmer grumbled, "Life is lousy, not worth getting out of bed for." God was listening to the conversation and thought, "Lousy? You think your life is lousy now? I'll show you what lousy is."

The second farmer responded, "Life is good, and God is generous. Each morning when I awaken, I'm grateful for the gift of another day." God smiled when he heard the second man's words and thought, "Good? You think your life is good now? I'll show you what good is."

While I cringe at this description of how God works, I like how the story highlights a relational dividend to our expressions of gratitude. Expressing appreciation to others maintains a two-way relational movement between giver and recipient and draws us toward our source of gratitude. The woman in our story certainly experienced this; her expression of gratitude propelled her toward Jesus and resulted in His assurance that her sins were forgiven. Great as her gratitude to Jesus was when she entered Simon's home, their exchange surely deepened it.

Weekly worship becomes an expression of gratitude, as we respond to God's initiative and character by proclaiming His goodness. Giving generously of our financial resources is another way of acknowledging and responding to God's generosity; we acknowledge that what we have ultimately came from His hand rather than originating from ours. The more avenues we can identify to express thanks to the Lord and to others, the more deeply we'll carve a spirit of gratitude within. As Henri Nouwen noted, **"Every time we decide to be grateful it will be easier to see new things to be grateful for.** Gratitude begets gratitude, just as love begets love."

How can you express gratitude this week?

Gratitude When It's Hard
Before concluding, let's acknowledge experiences and circumstances—even seasons—for which we're *not* grateful. In moments that we wish were different, gratitude seems out of place. Since

none of us are immune from such times, how do they fit into a spirit of gratitude? Let's answer that question by looking to our Lord's example during a horrible experience the night before He went to the cross:

> While they were eating, Jesus took bread, gave thanks and broke it, and gave it to his disciples, saying, "Take it; this is my body."
> Then he took the cup, gave thanks and offered it to them, and they all drank from it (Mark 14:22-23).

Our Lord understood that the hours ahead would be incredibly painful; His later prayers in Gethsemane reveal a dread of what lay before him. Yet Jesus' final meal with His disciples before He was crucified contains an element that I missed for years. The first three Gospels tell us that when Jesus took the bread and cup—the very elements representing the agony that awaited—He gave thanks for each. How can this be?

Jesus' words of thanks were rooted in His understanding that God was doing more than could be seen in that moment. Our Lord trusted in the good that His Father could bring from the pain He would experience; this trust enabled Jesus to say thank you to God even in the worst of moments. His example encourages us to thank God not only for the good, but also for painful or challenging circumstances. Obviously, we often won't understand reasons for our suffering the way Jesus did at the table with His disciples. But the Apostle Paul admonished us, "Give thanks in all circumstances" (I Thessalonians 5:18). Easy to say, hard to do—but to his credit, Paul exemplified this attitude despite frequent persecutions and imprisonments.

Nouwen explained the importance of gratitude even in hard times:

"To be grateful for the good things that happen in our lives is easy, but to be grateful for all of our lives—the good as well as the bad, the moments of joy as well as the moments of sorrow, the successes as well as the failures, the rewards as well as the rejections—that requires hard spiritual work.

Still, we are only grateful people when we can say thank you to all that has brought us to the present moment. As long as we keep dividing our lives between events and people we would like to remember and those we would rather forget, we cannot claim the fullness of our beings as a gift of God to be grateful for."

When life is going well, gratitude's roots may remain shallow and undeveloped. But challenges and difficulties, in their own perverse way, drive roots of gratitude deeper out of necessity. We can either rise above what we're experiencing or get plowed under. Sometimes, gratitude may be the only thing we'll have a choice about. Even if our gratitude in hard places is meager, it becomes an expression of trust in God's love and care, and in His promise and power to redeem. It's a declaration of faith that our Lord's story is bigger than we can see, and our hope that we might, someday, see some benefit to our challenges.

I saw this beautifully expressed a few years ago when preaching before Thanksgiving about Jesus' thankful response at the table. After the sermon, I invited worship participants to write on a card words that represented a hard place they were willing to give thanks to God for. As an act of worship, they were encouraged to bring these cards forward during our closing song. I still have one card that we received that day, upon which someone wrote, "Life is hard. I am thankful for the hard. Thank you, Lord."

How can you maintain a spirit of gratitude even in challenging circumstances?

<u>Final Thought</u>
Martin Rinkart was a German pastor who ministered in the seventeenth century during the Thirty Years' War. It resulted in famine and plague, and Rinkart was left to care for an entire village after two other local ministers died. His wife was among 8,000 who died during just one year. Amidst incredible pain and suffering, Rinkart wrote a table grace for his children that's become a faith-filled hymn of gratitude:

> Now thank we all our God
> With heart and hands and voices;
> Who wondrous things hath done,
> In whom his world rejoices.
> Who, from our mother's arms,
> Hath led us on our way
> With countless gifts of love
> And still is ours today.

Our attempts to say thank you to God, even when we cannot yet see reasons for gratitude, surely brings glory to Him. Rick Warren offered this caution against linking gratitude with circumstances:

> "I used to think that life was hills and valleys—you go through a dark time, then you go to the mountaintop, back and forth. I don't believe that anymore.
> Rather than life being hills and valleys, I believe that it's kind of like the rails on a railroad track, and at all

times you have something good and something bad in your life.

No matter how good things are in your life, there is always something bad that needs to be worked on.

And no matter how bad things are in your life, there is always something good you can thank God for."

Finishing well is enhanced by refusing to allow any "bad" rails to define our lives, and instead identifying and giving thanks for all the good that we also experience.

Chapter 8

EXPERIENCE PEACE IN LIFE'S UNCERTAINTIES

"The human race is a race of cowards, and I am not only marching in that procession, but I'm carrying the banner."
— Mark Twain

When the United States defeated Japan on the island of Guam during World War II, a Japanese sergeant named Shoichi Yokoi retreated into a jungle cave, fearing capture. After American planes dropped leaflets announcing the war's end, Yokoi's fear of imprisonment kept him hidden in the jungle for the next 28 years. He hunted primarily at night during that time, living on rats, roaches, frogs and mangoes. Yokoi finally left the jungle in 1972 only after an altercation with local hunters prompted them to forcibly carry him out.

Fear motivates us in powerful ways; its sway is so great, only love more strongly influences our actions. Sometimes our fears are justified, exerting a positive influence. A fear of icy roads slows our driving speed. Fear of poisonous snakes and hot stoves prompts us to wisely keep our distance. Too often, though, fear motivates us in unhealthy ways, preventing us from experiencing life as fully as Jesus promises and we desire.

For one thing, fear prompts poor choices often resulting in regret or pain. A generation of Israelites missed out on experiencing the

Promised Land after their fearful response to the report of 10 of Moses' 12 spies. Peter's fear that his life was in danger caused him to deny Jesus three times, then weep bitterly about doing so. David's fear of consequences to his adultery with Bathsheba prompted him to order the death of her husband, who was among David's best soldiers; this act surely haunted David the remainder of his life. Even the Bible's first temptation played upon Adam and Eve's fear of missing out on something good, with disastrous results for all humanity.

Fear also chokes our spirit within, making it difficult to act. A Spanish priest in India named Carlos Valles witnessed this one day. Valles was bicycling through the Indian countryside when he noticed a strange stillness around him. Getting off his bike and looking around, Valles discovered a raised cobra with its hood spread, gazing at a small paralyzed bird on a nearby branch. Valles wrote:

> "I had heard that snakes do that to birds. Now I was seeing it. The bird had wings, but could not fly. It had a voice, but could not sing. It was frozen, stiff, mesmerized. The snake knew its own power and had cast its spell. The prey could not escape, though it had the whole sky for its range."

Valles intervened by waving his arms and shouting. The snake eventually lowered itself—and after it did, the bird found the power to fly away.

Fear comes in many forms. We may fear that financial resources won't keep pace with our years. Perhaps we fear physical limitations or poor health that could limit our independence or curtail activities we currently enjoy. Closely related, seeing others lack good quality of life during their final days can prompt us to fear a similar fate.

Finishing well goes hand in hand with a strong quality of peace within. Cultivating this peace along the journey of our years enables our pace forward to remain steady even when fear tugs at us. Roman philosopher Seneca wisely stated, "If we let things terrify us, life will not be worth living." Our next story of Mary, the mother of Jesus, provides a beautiful example of internal peace during external upheaval that dramatically changed her life.

Mary's Story

We're given few details about Mary's life; she was probably a young teenager when her story occurred, since girls commonly married at that age. Mary's wedding preparations with family and friends were one day jarred by an angel's appearance. Henry Ward Beecher wrote, "Of all miracles, there was none more sacred to a Hebrew than an angelic visitation." But this was not only a sacred moment, it was a life-changing one.

Our annual reading of the Christmas story leads us to expect this angel's appearance. However, Mary had no point of reference for it. The priest Zechariah had encountered an angel six months earlier, but his loss of speech likely kept that news from spreading. Before that, God had been silent for 400 years. This explains Luke's note that "Mary was greatly troubled" (1:29) by the angel's greeting:

> In the sixth month of Elizabeth's pregnancy, God sent the angel Gabriel to Nazareth, a town in Galilee, to a virgin pledged to be married to a man named Joseph, a descendant of David. The virgin's name was Mary. The angel went to her and said, "Greetings, you who are highly favored! The LORD is with you."

Mary was greatly troubled at his words and wondered what kind of greeting this might be. But the angel said to her, "Do not be afraid, Mary; you have found favor with God. You will conceive and give birth to a son, and you are to call him Jesus. He will be great and will be called the Son of the Most High. The LORD God will give him the throne of his father David, and he will reign over Jacob's descendants forever; his kingdom will never end."

"How will this be," Mary asked the angel, "since I am a virgin?"

The angel answered, "The Holy Spirit will come on you, and the power of the Most High will overshadow you. So the holy one to be born will be called the Son of God. Even Elizabeth your relative is going to have a child in her old age, and she who was said to be unable to conceive is in her sixth month. For no word from God will ever fail."

"I am the LORD's servant," Mary answered. "May your word to me be fulfilled." Then the angel left her. (Luke 1:26-38)

The angel's message was as startling as his sudden appearance. When I first learned I would be a father, the news initially took some time to sink in and I continued processing it the rest of the afternoon. We can only imagine how Mary's mind spun as she absorbed the angel's extraordinary news: *An angel was here; why did he come to me? I'm going to have a son; can this really be true? If so, what's this about him becoming king? And how can God produce a child within me?*

The angel's announcement was an earthshaking moment for both God's Kingdom and this young girl. Philip Yancey mused, "Nine months of awkward explanations, the lingering scent of scandal—it seems that God arranged the most humiliating circumstances possible for his entrance, as if to avoid any charge of favoritism." A once-in-a-lifetime experience, exciting in any other setting, now invited ridicule and social isolation as Mary anticipated sharing her news with others. Because the rarity of angelic visits made Mary's encounter sound far-fetched, others would logically conclude that her pregnancy was the result of promiscuity. Joseph's initial decision to divorce Mary revealed his disbelief of her story. Mary had to wonder how her parents would receive her news of a pregnancy.

Despite the angel's promises, this encounter created an uncertain future for Mary. Fear could have easily taken over, which makes Mary's response to the angel's announcement so remarkable. Sarah laughed upon hearing God's promise of a child. Gideon asked for a sign before doing what God asked of him. Zechariah questioned how he could be certain of the angel's words. Many today refuse to accept the biblical account of Mary's virgin birth because it's not rational or natural. Mary simply stated, "I am the Lord's servant. May your word to me be fulfilled" (Luke 1:38).

Webster's Dictionary describes peace as, "A state of calm and quiet." Perhaps Mary's calm, trusting response to the chaos breaking into her life is what prompted God to trust this young girl to raise His Son with the godliness and care that Jesus deserved. Let's consider how we can experience this peace that we see in Mary.

Our story

When Italian poet Dante Alighieri visited a monastery, a Franciscan friar greeted him with the question, "What do you wish?" Dante answered with just one word: "Peace." In contrast to Mary's calm response, fear grips us more frequently than we'd like. Fear sometimes keeps us awake at night. Fear can accompany us throughout the day, despite our best attempts to shake it off. Words like "cancer" or "divorce" immediately trigger fear, as does any uncertainty about our circumstances, loved ones, or the future. Fear for legitimate reasons is hard enough; our imagination can fuel fears that lack substance but knock us off balance no less. Mark Twain noted this when he wrote, "I'm an old man, and I've seen a lot of troubles in my lifetime that never happened."

When our minds are consumed and hearts shaken by fear, we long for a calm and stabilizing peace within. For more than 30 years, I've kept a *Los Angeles Times* newspaper article about Cambodian refugees in Southern California who experienced fear-inducing earthquakes in their new homeland. My reason for saving it all these years is a highlighted quote in the sub-caption: "**All we want is peace of mind, but we don't know how to get it.**" Those words reflect the cry of the human heart. With reasons for fear seemingly on the increase, how can we experience peace that holds us fast? Mary's internal calm in the face of external turbulence provides an example of what's possible. Let's explore three ways of cultivating a steady source of peace along our journey of finishing well.

1. Build Christ's Presence Within

A legend from India described a mouse that was afraid of cats and convinced a magician to change her into a cat. This addressed her fear, until she encountered a dog. At her request, the magician changed her into a dog, and all was fine . . . until she met a tiger. Once again, the magician agreed to change her into what she most feared. She was happy as a tiger until eventually encountering a hunter. After again approaching the magician, he refused to make another change, explaining, "I will make you into a mouse again, for though you have the body of a tiger, you still have the heart of a mouse."

Like this mouse, we often associate peace with managing our

external circumstances. We try to keep life on an even keel, as if we can influence or control life's disruptive surprises. We go out of our way to avoid rocking the boat with others, even when conflict keeps us churning within. Lasting peace is developed internally, not managed externally; at best, the latter simply postpones fear until the next storm cloud looms. Mary modeled a calm inward response that rose above the news jolting her life. Years later, her son offered a promise of peace when Jesus said, "**Peace I leave with you; my peace I give you. I do not give to you as the world gives. Do not let your hearts be troubled and do not be afraid**" (John 14:27).

The internal peace that Jesus offered had nothing to do with external circumstances. Jesus spoke these words on the night He was betrayed, when His disciples experienced tremendous turmoil. They had already learned that one in their midst was a traitor, and the most loyal member would three times deny knowing Jesus. After devoting three years of their lives to following Jesus, they were told He was leaving, and that they couldn't follow. Our Lord knew they would also soon see Him arrested and beaten, then executed in the cruelest way possible.

Understanding that He couldn't spare His disciples the turbulence about to rock their lives, Jesus promised a peace that could anchor their hearts. Christ's statement that he didn't give as the world did contrasted His peace with the futile efforts of many who pursue peace. That's because Jesus' promise of peace is never dependent upon smooth or temporary circumstances. The disciples heard these words amidst a world turning upside down, and they would soon scatter in confusion and fear. Jesus offered a peace that would hold them fast when their lives *weren't* calm.

When a contest invited artists to paint a picture of peace, the entries were eventually narrowed to two. One artist portrayed peace with a quiet lake high in the mountains. In contrast, the other artist painted a thundering waterfall, with a tree branch extended over the roaring water. On the branch sat a robin, wet with spray, sitting undisturbed on her nest. That's a wonderful image of the peace Jesus promises us. It won't calm our circumstances; it *will* calm us, anchoring us internally even when life rages externally.

This sounds great—but if we read further, we'd discover that Jesus' promise of peace didn't initially stick. When His disciples were next seen together three days later, they had the "doors locked for fear of the Jews" (John 20:19). It wasn't until the resurrected Christ joined them, followed later by the Holy Spirit's influence, that these men finally experienced the peace promised by Jesus. This reminds us that peace comes not from Christ's assurance, but from His presence and influence within. Fear is triggered by circumstances that seem larger than us; Christ's peace flows from confidence that God is bigger and able to hold us fast in every circumstance. The following quote has been used by so many that I'm not sure who said it first—but it bears repeating: "**Peace is not the absence of trouble. Peace is the presence of God.**"

To experience Christ's peace, we need to remain close to Him. We do this by spending regular time with Jesus, seeking to better know the One who can hold us fast in peace, and cultivating a growing awareness of His constant presence and help. As we turn to and experience this peace, the psalmist's words can become our own: "**He delivered me from all my fears**" (Psalm 34:4).

How can you cultivate a closeness with Jesus that enables you to experience His peace?

2. Bring Fears to God

The summer after my first year of college, a new job became a source of anxiety. About the same time, I discovered a promise that provided constant encouragement throughout this experience:

> Do not be anxious about anything, but in every situation, by prayer and petition, with thanksgiving, present your requests to God. And the peace of God, which transcends all understanding, will guard your hearts and your minds in Christ Jesus (Philippians 4:6-7).

Let's be honest: bringing places of anxiety to God isn't always our first instinct. How often have we repeated the same routine when fear clutches our hearts? We become fixated upon looming threats, allowing our minds to repeatedly replay worst-case scenarios (we do this especially well in the middle of the night). Each time this pattern repeats itself, fear wears us down a bit more. We accomplish nothing, and only later does it occur to us to bring our fear to God as a child would with a parent. Better to bring our fears to God before slipping into this futile process. Though reasons for fear won't magically disappear when we do, our hearts can experience His rest sooner rather than later. This leads to a second element and promise of this passage.

Paul assures us that God's peace will guard our hearts and minds—places within where fear tends to reside. The Greek word here means to "stand guard over." Paul offered an image familiar to his audience: Philippi was a Roman military garrison where soldiers were constantly observed in this position. In the same way that they prevented unauthorized access, Paul encourages us that God's peace can prevent fear's unsettling influence from taking root within our hearts and minds.

Paul also declares that God's peace "transcends all understanding." Some scholars believe Paul means that this peace is so vast, we can't fully comprehend it. I like to think it also means that we experience Christ's peace when it's least anticipated, in moments and places when fear is expected to have its way. I frequently see this when visiting church members who are hospitalized or dying. These can be fearful moments, yet I'll often encounter a posture of peace. Just last week I visited a church member of more than seventy-five years, who wasn't far from death. When I asked if she was anxious about what lay ahead, she looked at me like I was crazy and responded, "Why should I be? I'm a Christian!" As we bring our fears to God, He can keep our hearts and minds calmer than our efforts can achieve.

What fears have you been churning on lately, that you can bring to God?

3. Understand Deeper Fears

Most of us could quickly name some of our most common fears. But we often overlook the tremendous impact that other, less obvious, fears have upon our choices and approach to life. Fears deep within can be shaped by childhood trauma or other painful life experiences; they may also be triggered by our reaction to situations we never again want to experience. Fears outside our self-awareness can exert tremendous influence upon how we live, and our inability to name these fears prevents us from addressing them in constructive ways.

When I counsel couples before marriage, I use an image of turning over rocks and exploring what's underneath to describe our conversation about their relationship. As we examine their relational dynamics, couples often nod knowingly or smile at each other, indicating that certain issues aren't a surprise. Sometimes though, I'll see a startled reaction to some new revelation that one of them hadn't previously known—and I'll know I've done my job by bringing it to light so they can discuss it. **Identifying fears beneath the surface enables us to address them proactively rather than experience them reactively.**

Remember the JoHari Window in Chapter 5? This illustration of knowledge we've yet to learn about ourselves also includes unknown fears that can detrimentally influence us. Fortunately, our Creator is fully aware of these fears; even better, He wants to enlarge our understanding of them when we seek His knowledge and perspective. As we discover and face previously unknown fears, we can better understand their impact upon us. My experience a few years ago illustrates how we can reduce fear's power when we address it head-on.

My greatest fear for much of my life has been rattlesnakes; this was shaped by a few encounters with them while growing up, coupled with an active imagination. When Deborah and I moved across town three years ago, we were delighted to discover the large Ute Valley Park nearby with many great hiking trails. Then I saw the signs warning of rattlesnakes in the park. The first few weeks in our new location, my fear kept me out of the park and off the inviting trails—even though it was winter, when snakes hibernate! Once my desire to explore these trails forced me to face this fear, I eventually got beyond a fear of rattlesnakes waiting to attack as I walked by. Instead, I now understand that they're more afraid of me than I of them. I've seen one rattlesnake in the park and may have closer encounters with others in the years ahead. But addressing and reducing this fear that had grabbed my heart for so many years has been wonderfully freeing.

Would you invite God to reveal fears of which you're unaware, that may be impacting you?

Final Thought

Thirty years ago, I took a group of single adults at my church on an eight-day backpacking trip in the Sierra Nevadas. I'd previously taken a similar trip with the company guiding us, so knew that we'd spend one day learning to climb up and repel down a rock face. Because of my previous experience, I looked forward to impressing the group, which included a woman I was dating.* When my turn came, I quickly began making my way up the rock face—but then slipped and fell. We were roped in from above, so I didn't fall far. However, it was still a disconcerting experience, and I scrambled to find another rock perch. After taking a few steps back up the rock, I fell again. I once again retreated to the foothold I'd previously discovered, and this time refused to move from it. Though my two falls hadn't caused any physical harm, my heart and mind were another matter. I was afraid of falling again; I was also afraid of being stuck where I was. It was not one of my better leadership moments.

Fortunately, I eventually trusted the instruction of our guide at the top of the rock, who coached me to unseen ledges. She helped me move from my fear-driven stuck position, to eventually get where I wanted to be. I find this a helpful illustration of how God's Holy Spirit works within us when we're knocked off balance and fearful. His reassuring presence encourages us that we're not alone in our fear. His direction provides hope in a way forward beyond what we can see. Most important, He becomes our source of peace that holds us together internally when we're buffeted externally.

Before going to the cross, Jesus promised peace to His disciples. Though they didn't experience it immediately, they eventually overcame their fear, boldly speaking in public and willingly enduring threats and even death. If God could take a room of frightened followers and so radically transform their fearful hearts, He can meet you in this important element of finishing well.

*Fortunately, I still got the girl, as she overlooked my climbing ineptitude and later married me.

PART III
LOOKING UP

Chapter 9

WAITING ON GOD'S TIMING

"Above all else, trust in the slow work of God."
— Teilhard de Chardin

The California Newspaper Association described a small-town newspaper's disastrous attempts to correct an error in its classified ads:

(Monday) "FOR SALE—R.D. Jones has one sewing machine for sale. Phone 948-0707 after 7 p.m. and ask for Mrs. Kelly who lives with him cheap."

(Tuesday) "NOTICE—We regret having erred in R.D. Jones' ad yesterday. It should have read: One sewing machine. Cheap. Phone 948-0707 and ask for Mrs. Kelly who lives with him after 7 p.m."

(Wednesday) "NOTICE—R.D. Jones has informed us that he has received several annoying telephone calls because of the error we made in his classified ad yesterday. His ad stands correct as follows: FOR SALE—R.D. Jones has one sewing machine for sale. Cheap. Phone 948-0707 p.m. and ask for Mrs. Kelly who loves with him."

(Thursday) "NOTICE—I, R.D. Jones, have NO sewing

machine for sale. I SMASHED IT. Don't call 948-0707, as the telephone has been disconnected. I have NOT been carrying on with Mrs. Kelly. Until yesterday she was my housekeeper, but she quit."

Things don't always go as planned. Sometimes this results in minor inconvenience, like the aborted sale of a sewing machine. Other times we become so knocked off balance, it's difficult to regain our footing. Jack Benny once remarked when accepting an award, "I really don't deserve this. But I have arthritis, and I don't deserve that either." As we've learned all too well by now, life surprises us with challenges we feel we don't deserve but must respond to anyway.

Our equilibrium can become jostled even more if we don't sense God's help in these moments. We're left waiting for both resolution to our needs and some encouraging sign of the Lord's response. Pastor Ben Patterson described this tension in *Waiting*:

> "Sometimes my whole family is sitting at the dinner table, ravenously hungry, and we are waiting for one child to finish washing up so we can say the blessing and begin eating. Then we hear him in the bathroom, singing idly, the water running in the sink as he dawdles his way to the kitchen, oblivious to our needs. Sometimes as I have waited, I have felt that God is that way—distracted and preoccupied and so wrapped up in his own affairs that he has forgotten about mine."

The Bible tells of many who had to wait for God. Abraham was promised a son, then waited 25 years for Isaac's birth. Joseph learned in a dream that he'd play an important role, but endured years of slavery and prison before experiencing it. The Lord broke

into David's young life with a promise that he'd be king, and he was—
23 years later. Then there are the psalmist's honest cries about the
slowness of God: "How long, O Lord? Will you forget me forever?
How long will you hide your face from me?" (Psalm 13:1)

A 93-year old blind church member I visited tearfully struggled
that her longing to go to heaven wasn't God's timing. I remember
my own tension with the Lord's slow assistance 25 years ago when
we moved from Florida to Colorado Springs. Though we faithfully
followed a clear call to change ministry settings, our condo in Florida
sat unsold for 6 months after our move. As we juggled two monthly
housing payments, I questioned why God wasn't in more of a hurry
to help us. Perhaps you've asked for relief from pain or discouraging
circumstances—and are still waiting. Or maybe you've prayed for
God's intervention with loved ones that still hasn't visibly occurred.
John Ortberg gave words to the tension we feel in these and other
moments:

> "Waiting may be the hardest single thing we are called to
> do. So it is frustrating when we turn to the Bible and find that
> God himself, who is all-powerful and all-wise, keeps saying
> to his people, 'Wait.' Forty-three times in the Old Testament
> alone, the people are commanded, 'Wait. Wait on the Lord.'"

As we seek to finish well, we want to maintain confidence in our
God who leads us forward. When we're surprised by dips and bends
along the way, we want to believe our Lord cares as much about them
as we do, and that He is actively involved in our journey. Our next
story is about a man named Jairus; though his wait was relatively
short, it offers encouragement when God doesn't seem to view our
needs as urgently as we do.

Jairus' Story

Luke's Gospel reveals three things about Jairus. First, he was a local synagogue ruler, which meant that he selected those who prayed, read scripture, and preached. This made Jairus an important man in his community. Second, we learn that he had one daughter. Finally, at the tender age of 12, she was near death. Any death is difficult to process; when it occurs at a young age, death shakes us even more. The pain of a parent who buries a child is hard to imagine—everything within cries out how wrong this feels. This possibility prompted Jairus to seek help from Jesus:

> Now when Jesus returned, a crowd welcomed him, for they were all expecting him. Then a man named Jairus, a synagogue leader, came and fell at Jesus' feet, pleading with him to come to his house because his only daughter, a girl of about twelve, was dying.
>
> As Jesus was on his way, the crowds almost crushed him. And a woman was there who had been subject to bleeding for twelve years, but no one could heal her. She came up behind him and touched the edge of his cloak, and immediately her bleeding stopped.
>
> "Who touched me?" Jesus asked.
>
> When they all denied it, Peter said, "Master, the people are crowding and pressing against you."
>
> But Jesus said, "Someone touched me; I know that power has gone out from me."
>
> Then the woman, seeing that she could not go unnoticed, came trembling and fell at his feet. In the presence of all the people, she told why she had touched him and how she had been instantly healed. Then he said to her, "Daughter, your

faith has healed you. Go in peace."

While Jesus was still speaking, someone came from the house of Jairus, the synagogue leader. "Your daughter is dead," he said. "Don't bother the teacher anymore." (Luke 8:40-49)

As a father, I've always been touched by this story. I remember first holding Matthew after his birth and instinctively thinking, "I would do anything for you." Once Suzanne was old enough to drive, my love for her made it hard to sleep soundly until she was home for the night. So, I feel for how incredibly difficult this experience was for Jairus.

There's also a fourth detail about Jairus that we're not told but can piece together: he was serving a God who wasn't providing the help Jairus was surely praying for. I'll never forget one Sunday when I had to lead our worship services following a family crisis earlier that morning. I smiled in front of our congregation that morning but was aching inside. I suspect Jairus experienced similar tension, proclaiming God's love and goodness to his congregation that he wasn't experiencing. We can only wonder how much Jairus' daughter's illness impacted his interaction with God. To what degree was Jairus' faith challenged, even as he spoke on God's behalf?

Approaching Jesus revealed Jairus' desperation, for the Gospels repeatedly describe a religious establishment at odds with Him. Perhaps Jairus rehearsed a calm request from one leader to another on his way to Jesus—but any anticipated dignity was overcome by despair when Jairus fell to the ground at Jesus' feet, begging for His help. It's not hard to imagine Jairus' relief when Jesus agreed to see his daughter, and the hope he felt as they started walking toward home.

But then Jesus stopped and began talking to someone else. We don't know whether His encounter with a woman in the crowd lasted five minutes or fifteen; it must have felt like hours to Jairus. I would have wanted to shout, "Jesus, I got you first—let's go!" Was Jairus tempted to tug Jesus away from this woman and get Him to his daughter as quickly as possible? While Jairus didn't interrupt, he surely churned inside during each agonizing moment he had to wait. Then a neighbor arrived with the news Jairus feared most: his daughter had died before Jesus saw her.

As the story continues, Jesus eventually healed this young girl— but Jairus didn't know this in that moment. All he could see was that Jesus seemingly hadn't valued his daughter's life as much as Jairus did. Christ didn't act with the same urgency Jairus felt—and perhaps because of that, his daughter was gone. Jesus insisted that He represented God; when He turned away from Jairus to another person, Jairus could naturally question God's concern about his need. And sometimes we're tempted to do the same.

Our Story

Phillips Brooks was a nineteenth-century preacher who wrote the words to *O Little Town of Bethlehem* and was known for his tremendous patience. A friend was surprised, therefore, to one day discover Brooks pacing back and forth in his study, obviously frustrated. When asked what was wrong, Brooks responded, "I'm in a hurry, but God is not!"

If our faith journey is long and deep, we may not question God's love and care when we're jarred by unexpected surprises. But the longer our prayers go unanswered, the more we can begin to wonder when or how we'll see reassurance of His involvement. A leper put words to our tension when he said to Jesus: "If you are willing, you can make me clean" (Mark 1:40). We know God *can* help us; when

He doesn't respond in a timely manner to needs that feel important to us, we become increasingly unsure of His *willingness* to help. German theologian Helmut Thielicke noted, "**The silence of God is the greatest test of our faith.**"

If someone we're scheduled to meet with doesn't show up, we naturally wonder if they took that time together as seriously as we did. Similar questions can arise around God's care when we don't see Him showing up in our circumstances. When Jesus turned away from Jairus to another need, Jairus could easily have assumed it was because Christ didn't care about his circumstances. Only time and further experience revealed that this wasn't the case. Jairus' story reminds us that God's perceived delay is never an indicator of disinterest. After all, He waited three days before raising His own Son from the grave.

God's timing is never arbitrary—there's always purpose and redemption in it. I'm grateful to a ministry colleague, Eunice McGarrahan, who illustrated God's responsiveness to our prayers with an equilateral triangle. Picture the left side of this triangle representing our prayers to God, and the right side His answers. The bottom of the triangle, from left to right, reflects the time we must walk through between our prayers and when we see our Lord's answers. Like Jairus, we only see partway into our story, leaving us wondering at times when or how the Lord will help us.

Let's consider five brief thoughts that can encourage us as we wait on God's timing.

• **What God does within us as we wait is sometimes of greater importance than what we're waiting for.**

When biblical characters had to wait for what God promised, it wasn't because His timing was arbitrary, or He'd forgotten. There was often more that the Lord wanted to do within them or others around them while they waited, before fulfilling His promise. God will often use the pain and suffering we want to flee from to carve out deeper places within us. Richard Hendrix stated, **"Second only to suffering, waiting may be the greatest teacher and trainer in godliness, maturity, and genuine spirituality most of us ever encounter."**

- **God can accomplish more in His timing than we're waiting for.**

The assistance that we impatiently await may be smaller at times than what God wants to accomplish. After all, Paul reminded us that God is "able to do *immeasurably* more than *all* we ask or *imagine*" (Ephesians 3:20, emphasis mine). Martin Luther stated, "We pray for silver, but God often gives us gold instead." That's not something we should expect, but it's a helpful reminder that our Lord often has bigger designs than we can anticipate. The cross provides a powerful example. As Christ's disciples wondered how they would survive the death of their leader, God was redeeming His people through Jesus' willing sacrifice.

- **God waits for us far more often than we wait for Him.**

As we impatiently await God's intervention, wondering why He won't hurry, we give little thought to how much He waits for us. Our Lord frequently waits for greater responsiveness in our relationship with Him. God waits for us to enjoy and fully use gifts that He gives us; while writing these words, I sensed Him waiting for me to stop and enjoy the beautiful sunrise He provided. He also waits for us to more willingly be His light and salt in a world desperately in need of it. Archbishop Anthony Bloom noted:

> "We stand before God and we shout into an empty sky, out of which there is no reply. We turn in all directions and He is not to

be found. What ought we to think of this situation? . . .

"God could complain about us a great deal more than we about Him. We complain that He does not make Himself present to us for the few minutes we reserve for Him, but what about the twenty-three and a half hours during which God may be knocking at our door and we answer 'I am busy' . . . or do not answer at all because we do not even hear the knock at the door of our heart . . . We have no right to complain of the absence of God, because we are a great deal more absent than He ever is."

- **A lack of tension while waiting for God could indicate lowered expectations of Him**.

Our desire to avoid disappointment often prompts us to lower our expectations of God. After all, if we expect less of Him, we're less likely to become disappointed by His timing or inactivity. Author Philip Yancey described one reader's honest acknowledgement: "I guess I've been disappointed enough times that I simply pray for less and less in order not to be disappointed over and over." Perhaps this provides helpful clarity around our waiting on God. We *want* to experience tension with His timing, for as hard as that feels, it's a sign that we still have high expectations of our Lord. Waiting upon God is a courageous act of faith.

- **We wait upon God actively, not passively**.

Henri Nouwen described the posture of actively waiting:

"Most of us think of waiting as something very passive, a hopeless state determined by events totally out of our hands. The bus is late? You cannot do anything about it, so you have to sit there and just wait.

But there is none of this passivity in scripture. Those who are waiting are waiting very actively. They know that what they are waiting for is growing from the ground on which they are standing. That's the secret. The secret of waiting is the faith that the seed has been planted, that something has begun."

How can we actively wait upon God, especially in difficult moments when we lack reassuring signs of his presence and activity? Two actions can help.

1. Shift the Focus

When God's timing is slower that we prefer, we instinctively gaze at our watches and calendars—*our* measurements of time, against which God often comes up woefully short. As Eugene Peterson astutely put it, "Our compulsive timetables collide with God's leisurely providence. We tell God not only what to do but when to do it." We then become increasingly discouraged or frustrated when He doesn't act in what we consider a timely manner. Given all our options today for immediate results, **the contrast between our expectations of quick relief and God's deliberate timing have never been greater**. Our ancestors thought nothing of taking weeks to travel across the United States; we wait impatiently at long traffic lights or in slow lanes at the store.

While waiting on God's timing, our gaze is better placed upon His character. Roman philosopher Cicero stated, "The gods attend to great matters; they neglect small ones." But this is never true of our God. Scripture repeatedly assures us that the Lord is actively at work in our lives. Even when we can't sense God's help during challenging circumstances, we can hold fast to our understanding of who He is. When the passage of time suggests that God isn't interested in helping us, His self-revelation provides a different and more accurate perspective.

What about God's character is helpful to remember when you're waiting for Him to act?

2. Honestly Communicate Tension

Spiritual questions and uncertainties can become toxic within if left unaddressed; they gradually and silently erode our confidence in the very One we're looking to for help. **Questions about God's activity aren't enemies of our faith, but healthy expressions of it.** We see this in the Psalms, when frustrated cries to God often led individuals to a different place with Him by the end of their prayers than when they'd started. I admire the honesty of Lewis Smedes, who prayed following the death of a child, "Oh, Lord, my God. You set me up. You promised to be with us, not once in awhile, but always. But not today."

Old Testament scholar Walter Brueggemann suggested that our faith goes through three stages. Our relationship with God begins with a focus upon security, and we count on Him to provide for us. Then, at some point along the way, we become knocked off balance by life events that shatter this trust. Finally, according to Brueggemann, we regain our spiritual equilibrium, developing a deeper understanding of what it means to be in relationship with God. Engaging God honestly about His seeming lack of responsiveness can draw us closer to Him in the long run.

We usually feel most comfortable when we're in control of our circumstances. But waiting always occurs from a posture of *not* being in control. To quote Nouwen again:

> "For many people, waiting is an awful desert between where they are and where they want to go. And people do not like such a place. They want to get out of it by doing something. . . Fearful people have a hard time waiting, because when we are afraid we want to get away from where we are."

How do you communicate to God your frustration or questions about His timing?

Final thought

Russell Kelfer beautifully captured our tension and our Lord's intentionality in this poem:

Desperately, helplessly, longingly, I cried.
Quietly, patiently, lovingly, He replied.
I pleaded, and I wept for a clue to my fate,
And the Master so gently said, "Child you must wait."

"Wait? You say wait?" my indignant reply.
"Lord I need answers, I need to know why.
Is your hand shortened? Or have you not heard?
By faith I have asked, and I'm claiming your word.

"My future and all to which I relate
Hangs in the balance, and you tell me to 'wait?'
I'm needing a 'yes,' a go-ahead sign,
Or even a 'no,' to which I can resign.

"You promised, dear Lord, that if we believe,
We need but to ask, and we shall receive.
And Lord, I've been asking, and this is my cry:
I'm weary of asking! I need a reply."

Then quietly, softly, I learned of my fate
As my Master replied again, "You must wait."
So I slumped in my chair, defeated and taut
And grumbled to God: "So I'm waiting for what?"

He seemed then to kneel and His eyes met with mine
And He tenderly said, "I could give you a sign.
I could shake the heavens and darken the sun
I could raise the dead and cause mountains to run.

"I could give all you seek, and pleased you would be.
You'd have what you want, but you wouldn't know me.
You'd not know the depth of My love for each saint;
You'd not know the power that I give to the faint.

"You'd not learn to see through clouds of despair;
You'd not learn to trust, just by knowing I'm there.
You'd not know the joy of resting in Me,
When darkness and silence was all you could see.

"You would never experience the fullness of love
When the peace of My Spirit descends like a dove.
You would know that I give, and I save, for a start,
But you'd not know the depth and the beat of My heart.
"The glow of My comfort late in the night;

The faith that I give when you walk without sight;
The depth that's beyond getting just what you ask
From an infinite God who makes what you have last.

"You'd never know, should your pain quickly flee,
What it means that 'My grace is sufficient for thee.'
Yes, your dearest dreams overnight could come true,
But oh, the loss, if you missed what I'm doing in you.

"So be silent, my child, and in time you will see
That the greatest of gifts is to truly know Me.
And though oft' My answers seem terribly late,
My most precious answer of all is still . . . wait."

We'll all experience moments when God's timing is different from ours. Difficult as these seasons of waiting are, they can teach us more about our Lord and about us. Equally important, they help us finish well by developing greater trust in the Lord's leading for the journey still ahead. The next time you're partway through your story, wondering why your needs don't seem as urgent to God as they are to you, remember Jairus' story and the lesson it offers: **God's perceived delay is never an indicator of His disinterest.**

Chapter 10

FIND STRENGTH IN MOMENTS OF WEAKNESS

"The American Dream is to live in our strength; God's dream is that we live in our weakness."

— Mike Erre

Max Lucado tells this story in *Eye of the Storm*:

Chippy the Parakeet never saw it coming. One second he was peacefully perched in his cage minding his own business. The next he was sucked in, washed up, and blown over.

The problem began when Chippy's owner decided to clean Chippy's cage with a vacuum cleaner. She removed the attachment from the end of the hose and stuck it in the cage. The phone rang and she turned to pick it up. She'd barely said "hello" when "sssop!" Chippy got sucked in.

The bird owner gasped, put down the phone, turned off the vacuum, and opened the bag. There was Chippy—still alive, but stunned.

Since the bird was covered with dust and soot, she grabbed him and raced to the bathroom, turned on the faucet and held Chippy under the running water. Then, realizing that Chippy was soaked and shivering, she did what any compassionate bird owner would do: she reached

for the hair dryer and blasted the pet with hot air.

Poor Chippy never knew what hit him.

A few days after the trauma, the reporter who'd initially written about the event contacted Chippy's owner to see how the bird was recovering. "Well," she replied, "Chippy doesn't sing much anymore—he just sits and stares."

Like Chippy, life's surprises can steal the song from our hearts. Looking over our congregation during worship one Sunday, I identified these challenging circumstances:

- Someone was caring for both a spouse in poor health and an aging parent;
- Someone was experiencing the beginning stages of dementia;
- Someone was grieving the death of a spouse and longing for a new one;
- Someone was battling cancer;
- One couple was experiencing physical and financial repercussions from a car accident that wasn't their fault;
- Two people were reeling from bad endings to long-time jobs;
- Two parents were grieving their son's divorce, while another two were supporting their daughter who was experiencing deep depression;
- Grandparents were raising a grandchild amidst added challenges from the child's parent;
- One person's life was dramatically altered by a sudden brain injury, while another was experiencing limitations from a stroke. Someone else had lupus, another had cerebral palsy, and a third person had multiple sclerosis.

You get the idea. And those were just situations I knew of that morning. None of us are immune from overwhelming challenges and painful disappointments. Allen Saunders was the first of many to note, "Life is what happens to us while we are making other plans." We learn how to rise to challenges as we move through life, gaining experience and confidence along the way, and those lessons serve us well during later years. However, the further we advance into what Walter Wright refers to as the third third of our lives, the more easily we can feel knocked off balance and vulnerable. Sudden losses or difficulties can make us less certain of our ability to adequately cope and respond.

When we envision finishing well, we anticipate a posture of strength. But life doesn't always accommodate that desire, and we're sometimes forced to learn new lessons about weakness. Therefore, **finishing well includes acceptance that we won't always be at our best.** We want to give ourselves grace in such moments, as well as develop a source of strength that we can lean upon. David's story offers an encouraging reminder that moments of weakness we would rather avoid often position us to experience more of God.

David's Story

The prophet Samuel anointed David king during the tenth century B.C. when he was a young boy. This would have been a great career move at another time. However, Saul was still firmly entrenched as Israel's king, and repeatedly sought to kill David during the following years. Though David continually eluded Saul, several close calls eventually prompted him to flee Israel and seek protection from a neighboring Philistine king. David earlier attempted the same action, barely escaping with his life, so this second attempt revealed his desperation. Adding to his peril, David sought refuge in the territory of the giant warrior Goliath, who he had previously killed. The Philistines' willingness to provide protection seems surprising, but Saul's relentless pursuit of David made Israel's enemy their ally. David and his men were given the abandoned city of Ziklag that the Philistines had previously captured from Israel, and Saul was forced to halt his pursuit.

David carried out an elaborate scheme during the following months. He and his men raided tribes to the south that were long-time enemies of Israel, killing any witnesses to their location. David then told the Philistine king that they had raided Israelite villages and shared the plunder with him. Everyone was happy: David was safe, the king benefited from his protection, David's men and their families had a home, and Israel gained a buffer where David and his men raided.

Unfortunately, David's deception worked too well; he and his men eventually ended up on the wrong side of an approaching battle with Israel. They were saved from fighting their countrymen when other Philistine leaders protested that these transplanted Israelites could turn on them in battle. Instead, David and his men were sent home:

> David and his men reached Ziklag on the third day. Now the Amalekites had raided the Negev and Ziklag. They had attacked Ziklag and burned it, and had taken captive the women and everyone else in it, both young and old. They killed none of them, but carried them off as they went on their way.
>
> When David and his men reached Ziklag, they found it destroyed by fire and their wives and sons and daughters taken captive. So David and his men wept aloud until they had no strength left to weep. David's two wives had been captured—Ahinoam of Jezreel and Abigail, the widow of

Nabal of Carmel. David was greatly distressed because the men were talking of stoning him; each one was bitter in spirit because of his sons and daughters. But David found strength in the LORD his God. (I Samuel 30:1-6)

Once David and his men saw smoke in the distance, their pace undoubtedly quickened with growing anxiety at what they would find. The group's arrival home confirmed their greatest fears: everyone dear to them had been captured and all they possessed burned. The discovery was so devastating, we're told, "David and his men wept aloud until they had no strength left to weep" (30:4). Literally, they wept to the point of exhaustion. Ironically, David's village was attacked by one of the groups he and his men had raided, and they now experienced what they had previously afflicted upon others. Each man understood that their family members were likely on their way to Egyptian slave markets.

As the loss sank in, grief turned to bitterness, then anger. What may at first have been a whispered thought began spreading among the men: David deserved death for their loss. For one thing, he was responsible for leaving the village unprotected. Additionally, David could have killed Saul on two previous occasions and become king, but refused his men's urging to do so; some likely felt this loss could have been avoided if he'd listened to them. Finally, the character of David's followers added to his danger. We're told a few chapters earlier, "All those who were in distress or in debt or discontented gathered around (David), and he became their leader" (I Samuel 22:2). Chuck Swindoll's description of David's men seems appropriate:

"They all had one thing in common—a bad record . . .

They were so tough they'd make Al Capone sleep with a night light . . . Anybody who got near the gang stayed as quiet as a roomful of nuns. They had a quaint name for those who crossed their paths . . . victims."

David had a lot to process: his heartache from losing all that was dear to him; his men's loss of faith in him; and his life at risk. Additionally, God's care and provision that he'd experienced on so many other occasions was nowhere to be seen. Given all these dynamics, it's not surprising to read, "David was greatly distressed" (30:6). What *is* surprising is the next sentence: "**But David found strength in the Lord His God" (I Samuel 30:6).** Though nothing about David's circumstances changed, something significant changed within him. A moment of weakness led to an experience of strength.

Amid devastating loss and threat of personal harm, *David found strength in the Lord his God.* These eight words suggest two counterintuitive actions by David. First, he clung to God who had just allowed this loss to occur. Don't underestimate how difficult this may have been. Setbacks that shake us and create need for God's strength also raise questions about why the One we're turning to allowed this to happen in the first place. Yet David turned for help to God in a moment when His goodness wasn't evident. Many of the psalmists model something similar, clinging to the very God they're questioning as they cry out to Him for answers.

Second, David turned to God immediately, rather than first relying upon his own best efforts. Again, this couldn't have been easy. David had two problems requiring immediate action. Pursuit needed to be quickly organized; every lost moment made loved ones harder to track and more susceptible to mistreatment. Even more pressing, David needed to provide a convincing argument why his men should keep him alive. Though David was tremendously resourceful, he made neither of these his first action. Instead, he turned to God. When he did, David found the strength he needed, not from his own best efforts but from His Lord. This strength enabled David to continue leading his men in recapturing their families and possessions.

Ernest Hemingway observed, "The world breaks everyone, and afterward many are strong at the broken places." This process provides a frequent template for novels: after a setback, the protagonist discovers resiliency and strength within to overcome a seemingly insurmountable challenge. But that's not the strength David experienced; his strength came from God. It gave David the emotional strength needed to rally his men, and the physical strength required to pursue and overcome the raiders. David's experience offers an encouraging reminder of the strength available to us during moments of weakness.

Our Story

It's difficult to relate to many stories about David, such as his defeat of Goliath or reign as king. But this story is different. More often than we'd prefer, each of our names could replace David's: "_____ was greatly distressed." Like Chippie, events surprise us in ways that choke our song. Like David's men, our reaction to loss can be exhausting. During moments of great discouragement, it's hard to imagine that our hearts will ever again feel light. New challenges associated with increasing years may feel overwhelming. Discouragement and weariness can grip our hearts as firmly as David experienced.

So, it's important to understand that God's strength sustains us during stormy uncertainty. It propels us through challenges that we may wonder if we're up to. God's strength provides His reassuring presence in moments of isolation, and His wisdom in seasons of uncertainty. When we experience tough times, the Lord wants us to find strength in Him like David did. Making David's experience our reality on the journey of finishing well becomes possible when we do three things.

1. Acknowledge Weakness

Near the end of my first year of ordained ministry I scheduled a 24-hour silent retreat. Shortly into this time, I became increasingly aware of my exhaustion from new responsibilities and necessary decisions that weighed heavily upon me. After a few hours of discouragement, I read Jesus' invitation, "Come to me, all you who are weary and burdened, and I will give you rest" (Matthew 11:28). Though this promise was familiar, it grabbed me in a new way that day: I heard Jesus naming how I felt. In response, I journaled the following prayer: *Lord, the burdens of my job seem so great, and my shoulders so small, that I have felt overwhelmed and discouraged these past few days.*

This acknowledgement made me feel better for a few minutes, until I realized that something more was needed to experience this promise. I began listing everything wearing me down, eventually identifying 13 decisions, conflicts and responsibilities. I then specifically prayed for each, acknowledging my need for God's help. Though this occurred nearly 30 years ago, I still remember feeling a weight lifted from that activity, and I returned to work with new strength to face these challenges. Since that retreat, I've continued finding strength in God during morning times together; after naming looming challenges that feel overwhelming, I'll ask for His power to respond well as I move through the day.

Acknowledging weakness isn't easy, for it goes against our instincts. We like to think we're capable and competent, and we regularly seek to convey that we're on top of things. Admitting weakness brings us face to face with our brokenness and neediness, which doesn't feel very good. But the uncomfortable reality is that we're more vulnerable and inadequate than we often prefer to admit. Fortunately, God assures us that undesirable places of weakness are opportunities to more fully experience His strength. One of my favorite promises in the Bible is God's declaration that "**my power is made perfect in weakness**" (II Corinthians 12:9). Yes, we'll always feel most comfortable in our strength, and God can use that for good. But it's in our weakness, where there's less of us, that we'll experience more of God. Moses certainly discovered this.

When God instructed Moses to lead the Israelites out of Egypt, he responded with repeated protests of inadequacy: "Who am I to do this?" "What should I tell them?" "What if they don't believe me?" "I can't speak well." While we find Moses' reticence unimpressive, something significant emerged from that conversation. God responded to each protest with assurances that He would make up the difference where Moses was lacking. But Moses only heard these encouraging words after first acknowledging his inadequacy. Finding strength in God requires similar admissions of weakness to ourselves and to our Lord.

What places of weakness can you acknowledge to God right now?

2. Lean Forward

Though I've lived in Colorado 25 years, I've never skied here; the only day I enjoyed this activity was in Washington shortly after college. It was fun, but I eventually decided to take up golf instead (courses were closer and the weather warmer). My one day on the slopes occurred more than 35 years ago, but I still recall an important lesson from it: successful skiing requires leaning forward. I probably remember this because it felt so counterintuitive as I hurtled downhill. Instinctively, I wanted to lean back toward the mountain as a safer posture, rather than away from it.

Leaning forward into the Lord during moments of weakness can also feel counter-intuitive, for two reasons. First, it can be hard to lean into God when our trust is shaken by trouble that He's allowed us to experience. During a recent five-week period, Deborah and I experienced back-to-back flight cancellations with the same airline just hours before we were to depart each flight. After the first cancellation, I half-expected that our airline would fail us again on our next flight. When it did, I had no confidence that it would get us home on our return flight (fortunately, it did). We can feel a similar lack of confidence in placing much weight of faith upon God when it appears that He's let us down and could again. But that's exactly what David did during his crisis. He leaned forward in faith when circumstances suggested that God might be uninterested or uninvolved. **Though David saw no signs of God's care and provision, he put the full weight of his faith upon His Lord.** God invites us to do the same.

A second challenge to leaning forward into God during moments of weakness stems from our self-sufficient instinct. When encountering a problem, our first response is to fix it. It often doesn't even occur to us to turn to God for strength until after we've finally exhausted our resources. We'd also rather depend upon ourselves than be dependent upon others. This not only delays our experience of what the Lord has to offer, it puts extra pressure on us to provide our own strength and solutions. Our efforts are certainly a necessary part of responding to challenges; after turning to God, David did eventually move to action. The key is moving in His direction and experiencing His strength sooner rather than later.

My wife has struggled for years with physical weakness of fibromyalgia and emotional weakness of depression. Knowing how easily she could become disillusioned with God because of these experiences, I've been inspired by how consistently Deborah leans into her Lord, clinging tightly to Him for the strength that she needs.

Yes, movement away from us towards God in times of weakness can feel as counter-intuitive as leaning forward down a mountain. But as we make this more a habit, we position ourselves to echo the prophet Isaiah's words, "**The Lord is my strength**" (Isaiah 12:2).

In what ways do you lean into God when troubles occur?

3. Wear out a path

When I was in first grade, the school bus dropped me off each afternoon near the home of family friends, where I stayed until my parents picked me up after work. I don't remember anything about my time with them, but I do remember the large field between their home and the bus stop. Rather than walking around the field, it was easier to cut through the middle of it. I obviously wasn't the first to discover this, for others had worn a path through the field that I could follow. This established route created a much easier trek at my young age than if I had forged my own path.

That path comes to mind when I think about David's story. Turning to God for strength was natural for David because he'd worn a path to the Lord prior to his crisis. The same principle is true for us. The more deeply we wear a path to God before difficulties arrive, the more easily and naturally we can run to Him when they do. But the opposite is also true. A well-worn path, neglected over time, can become less defined and more difficult to follow. Whether we've previously developed a worn path to God or need to begin doing so, today's movement along this path limits the emergence of spiritual weeds tomorrow that could make it harder to turn to Him when we need His strength.

I've been blessed to visit Israel five times, and each trip has included a tour of Masada. This mountain fortress in the desert was prepared by Herod the Great as a refuge in case of revolt or invasion. The word *Masada* comes from the Hebrew word "fortress", implying safety and security. The biblical reference to God as our fortress comes from this same root. Ken Gire noted, "Masada's are not built in times of trouble. They are peace-time projects, built and fortified in times of stability. If we wait until the upheaval to begin building, there won't be a fortress to run to when we need to." **Wearing out a path to our source of strength before we need it enables us to more easily turn to God when troubles suddenly surprise.**

In addition to regular patterns of prayer and reading our Bibles, weekly worship helps us regularly wear out a path to God. It reminds us of His promises of strength, and we affirm the Lord's power and goodness with our songs and prayers and are encouraged through sermons. I began this chapter with a list of people experiencing places of weakness one Sunday morning. Their challenges were different, but they all sought strength in God through worship that day. Though their hearts were heavy and hurting, they took initiative to be reminded anew of God's ability to meet their places of weakness. Regular times of worship can do the same for us.

In what ways are you currently wearing out a path to God—or if you're not, how can you?

Final Thought

Peggy Porter shared this story of a young boy who sought God's strength:

My son Gilbert was 8 years old and had been in Cub Scouts only a short time. During one of his meetings he was handed a sheet of paper, a block of wood and four tires and told to return home and give all to dad. That was not an easy task for Gilbert to do. Dad was not receptive to doing things with his son. But Gilbert tried. Dad read the paper and scoffed at the idea of making a pinewood derby car with his young, eager son.

The block of wood remained untouched as the weeks passed. Finally, mom stepped in to see if I could figure this all out. The project began. Having no carpentry skills, I decided it would be best if I simply read the directions and let Gilbert do the work. And he did. I read aloud the measurements, the rules of what we could do and what we couldn't do. Within days his block of wood was turning into a pinewood derby car. A little lopsided, but looking great (at least through the eyes of mom). Gilbert had not seen any of the other kids' cars and was feeling pretty proud of his "Blue Lightning," the pride that comes with knowing you did something on your own.

Then the big night came. With his blue pinewood derby in his hand and pride in his heart, we headed to the big race. Once there, my little one's pride turned to humility. Gilbert's car was obviously the only car made entirely on his own. All the other cars were a father-son partnership, with cool paint jobs and sleek body styles made for speed. A few of the boys giggled as they looked at Gilbert's lopsided, wobbly, unattractive vehicle. To add to the humiliation, Gilbert was the only boy without a man at his side. A couple of the boys who were from single parent homes at least had an uncle or grandfather by their side. Gilbert had "mom."

As the race began, it was done in elimination fashion. You kept racing as long as you were the winner. One by one the cars raced down the finely sanded ramp. Finally it was between Gilbert and the sleekest, fastest looking car there. As the last race was about to begin, my wide-eyed, shy 8-year-old asked if they could stop the race for a minute because he wanted to pray. The race stopped. Gilbert dropped to his knees, clutching his funny looking block of wood between his hands. With a wrinkled brow, he prayed in earnest for a very long minute and a half. Then he stood, smile on his face, and announced, "Okay, I am ready." Then he watched his block of wood wobble down the ramp with surprisingly great speed and rushed over the finish line a fraction of a second before the other boy's car.

Gilbert leaped into the air with a loud "Thank you" as the crowd roared in approval. The Cub Master came up to Gilbert with microphone in hand and asked the obvious question, "So you prayed to win, huh, Gilbert?" To which my young son answered, "Oh, no, sir. That wouldn't be fair to ask God to help you beat someone else. I just asked Him to make it so I don't cry when I lose."

Children seem to have a wisdom far beyond us. Gilbert didn't ask God to win the race. He didn't ask God to fix the outcome. Gilbert asked God to give him strength in the outcome.

In moments of weakness, strength is available from our heavenly Father—a strength that can hold us up and carry us forward in our efforts to finish well. For He promises, "Even to your old age and gray hairs, I am he, I am he who will sustain you. I have made you and I will carry you; I will sustain you and I will rescue you." (Isaiah 46:4).

Chapter 11

REFILL YOUR CUP

"For many of us the great danger is not that we will renounce our faith. It is that we will become so distracted and rushed and preoccupied that we will settle for a mediocre version of it. We will just skim our lives instead of actually living them."
— John Ortberg

Charles Price wrote of a high rise building that developed a significant crack on the 42nd floor a few years after opening. This prompted the building's owner to hire an architect to investigate the problem. When the building manager was informed of the architect's arrival, he took the elevator to the 42nd floor to meet her—but the architect was nowhere to be found. After a lengthy search, she was eventually discovered in the sixth basement.

The manager descended to that level and angrily asked the architect why she wasn't on the floor with the crack. The architect responded that while the crack was on the 42nd floor, the problem wasn't on that floor, but in the basement. Further investigation revealed that a building employee had wanted to build a garage at home but didn't have money or materials. He began visiting the sixth basement every evening after work, chiseling a brick from the wall that he took home in his lunchbox. After a few years of this practice, a crack eventually appeared on the 42nd floor.

Finishing well is fueled by a resilient spirit deep within. This source of joy and eagerness for life makes our journey easier but can also become thin over time. Depletion of our inner basement, brick by brick, eventually leads to external cracks that the world sees and to which we react. While our attention is naturally captured by these visible actions or attitudes, our focus is better spent identifying leakage beneath the surface that caused it. The challenge of prioritizing and remaining attentive to what's within us isn't unique to our later years but applies throughout our lifetime. And it makes a difference in our quality of finish.

Many are drawn to Psalm 23's encouraging imagery in the Old Testament. At one point the psalmist exclaimed, "my cup overflows" (Psalm 23:5). Who of us doesn't long to feel like our cup is overflowing, in what we're experiencing and how well we're doing? Too often, though, we seek to fill our cups with external reinforcements: relationships, experiences, purchases or comfort. These and other pursuits may initially create a sense of satisfaction or fullness within, but the effect rarely lasts. **A full and overflowing cup is only sustainable when our Lord is the source.** External circumstances are temporary, and our best efforts inconsistent. Only in God can we experience an ongoing deep, inward filling.

When we experience God's filling of our cups to overflowing, we're more likely to also experience the psalmist's declaration, "He restores my soul" (Psalm 23:3). The story of Mary and Martha illustrates postures that lead to both cup depletion and cup filling. These two women help us better understand what empties our cups within, and how we can proactively position ourselves to allow the Lord to refill them.

Mary's Story

Mary and Martha were followers of Jesus who also became His friends. The Gospel of John revealed the closeness of their relationship through Mary and Martha's interaction with Jesus about the death of their brother, Lazarus. Jesus' love for this family was evident in His tears upon arriving at Lazarus' tomb. It also prompted our Lord to bring Lazarus back to life.

The only other mention of these two sisters together occurred when Martha invited Jesus into her home. Though Martha sought to provide a warm welcome for their friend, she obviously wasn't enjoying His visit:

> As Jesus and his disciples were on their way, he came to a village where a woman named Martha opened her home to him. She had a sister called Mary, who sat at the Lord's feet listening to what he said. But Martha was distracted by all the preparations that had to be made. She came to him and asked, "Lord, don't you care that my sister has left me to do the work by myself? Tell her to help me!"
>
> "Martha, Martha," the Lord answered, "you are worried and upset about many things, but few things are needed—or indeed only one. Mary has chosen what is better, and it will not be taken away from her." (Luke 10:38-42)

When we host guests in our homes, we do our best to help them feel welcome. We may feel increased pressure to do this well if a visitor is a well-known public figure. Hospitality was a high priority in Jesus' time, and Martha seemingly attended to her friend's needs as conscientiously and responsibly as she could. But Martha's important activity took a toll, distracting her from the very One she was serving. There was obviously so much to be done, it prevented Martha from enjoying Jesus' company. Her cup was *not* overflowing, in contrast to her sister Mary.

Mary had surely cheerfully helped her sister host previous visitors. This time, though, she didn't lift a finger to help. Instead, her attention was fixed upon Jesus; she remained close to Him, taking in all that He said. It's not difficult to picture Martha periodically glaring at Mary the longer this went on. Perhaps she even started noisily slamming down dishes to remind her sister and others that *someone* was working. When Martha's subtle hints failed to generate any assistance, she resorted to confrontation. But rather than turn on her sister, Martha put Jesus in the middle. Essentially, she complained to Him, "Jesus, in light of all I'm doing for you, a little help getting my sister into the kitchen would be nice."

Jesus responded by acknowledging the stress that Martha was feeling. However, He didn't prod Mary with Martha's desired nudge to help her sister. Jesus didn't even praise Martha's hospitality; instead, He commended Mary's decision over Martha's. Perhaps Jesus' response was abrupt because He knew that's what Martha needed to hear. **Martha's activity and productivity were good, but they came at a cost.** It prevented her from enjoying Jesus' life-giving and cup-filling presence. In contrast, Mary chose to make the important value of hospitality secondary to her focus upon Jesus. While Jesus' response must have been deflating for Martha, He longed for her to experience Him in the same way as her sister.

Jesus' reinforcement of Mary and correction of Martha provides helpful encouragement to consider how our posture contributes to a cup that's either re-filling or becoming depleted.

Our Story

Three years ago, I became depleted in a way that I hadn't previously experienced and hope I never will again. The best way to describe it is that everything inside me felt deadened. I experienced a constant weariness within, and my emotions remained flat; nothing generated joy or excitement. Though I sought restoration in multiple ways, it was as if my cup had a leak and only filled to a certain point that was nowhere near the top. Over time I began to despair, unsure how or even if I could move to a better place. After experiencing this for about three months, Deborah and I went on a previously scheduled vacation to the ocean. As we left for a week, I wondered if I would be any better upon our return.

Nothing changed during the first three days of our trip, as I sat on the beach watching the waves, reading, thinking, and praying. On the fourth morning I was among the first to arrive on the beach, as was usually the case. When I did, I discovered that baby turtles had hatched from a nest in the sand and were instinctively making their way into the ocean. Because birds were swooping in to snatch them for an early breakfast, I was asked to help carry the laggards to the water (we normally weren't allowed to touch them). I picked up the one furthest behind and began walking it to the ocean. As I watched the little form crawling in my hands, God suddenly awakened something within me: I felt stirrings of joy and delight that had been absent for too long. In what felt like a sacred moment, I sensed the Lord's encouragement that things were going to be okay. From that point on, my cup within gradually started refilling.

After returning home, I began to better understand what had caused my inner depletion—and the dots weren't difficult to connect. My pace and activity the previous eight months had been more demanding than usual. Around the same time that some work responsibilities increased, we purchased a home across town and prepared ours of 21 years for sale. During a one-week period just two weeks before Christmas, we moved into our new home, unpacked, completed a final cleaning of our old home, and flew out of state for our son's wedding, which I performed. We then hosted our children during the week after Christmas, before moving back into the busyness of a new year. I faithfully responded to everything requiring my attention, but the cost was undetected leakage under the surface.

I've experienced internal depletion on many other occasions, though to a lesser degree, and this isn't unique to me. I suspect that the majority of those reading these words relate best to Martha in this story. We're responsible and conscientious, regularly juggling multiple competing demands and interests, and we generally do this well. If we had been in Martha's home that day, many of us would have joined her in the kitchen within minutes. Noise would have beckoned us that something needed to get done; guilt would have propelled us to do something about it. Wayne Muller stated, "Our culture invariably supposes that action and accomplishment are better than rest, that doing something—anything—is better than doing nothing."

But as I all too clearly learned during my difficult season, constant activity can deplete our cup over time. That's because busy lives aren't conducive to an overflowing cup within. Leighton Ford observed, "**There is a connection between our speed and the health of our spirit.**" With each new decade, our pace seems to quicken a bit more. What does it say about our country, that we have a mountain named "Rushmore?" Stress and weariness can become constant companions as we seek to keep up with the speed of society around us. Even as our activity slows with age, many of us pack more into our days than did the generation before us.

The increasing number of time-saving advances that we take advantage of should seemingly result in days that are less full. Our problem is that the time we save doesn't really create additional space in our lives. Instead, we too often fill saved time with more activity, resulting in lives that feel increasingly full. Henri Nouwen astutely noted, "Our lives often seem like overpacked suitcases bursting at the seams. In fact, we are almost always aware of being behind schedule . . . although we are very busy, we also have a lingering feeling of never really fulfilling our obligations."

In contrast, Mary didn't allow the urgency of nearby activity to keep her from becoming refilled by Jesus. She could only do this by more highly valuing a refilling of her cup in Christ's presence. Mary's example provides a breath of fresh air to our (and Martha's) approach. It also offers an example from which we can learn. Leighton Ford asserted, "**Most of us, if we are honest, are latter-day Martha's who deep inside are longing for some Mary time.**" This "Mary time" is key to sustaining us along our journey of finishing well. Therefore, let's explore three ways to position ourselves for a similar refilling of our cup.

1. Reassess Priorities

I started writing this chapter two weeks before beginning my sabbatical, which was a wonderful gift from my church. My goal was to complete this book by the end of this time away from work; however, this has prompted a growing tension between conflicting values. Chapter deadlines that I set during recent months pushed me along at a pace that achieved productivity, but at the cost of an increasingly depleted cup. Weeks consistently full from the relentless pace of writing left me feeling thin within. As a result, I was confronted with deciding between the greater good of two worthy pursuits: productivity, or a replenished cup within. **Like Martha,** we too often lean toward the easier tugs of life at the expense of richer Spirit-filling.

We usually recognize when our bodies need rest, but too often miss our need for God's replenishing rest within. Sometimes our focus on short-term results overrules the greater good of allowing God to fill our cup in ways He desires, and that we need. It's good to occasionally pause and assess whether activity is occurring at the expense of a depleted cup within. When that's the case, priorities should be examined, and change considered. Setting aside activity that's rewarding or enjoyable is never easy—but holding onto it may then require us to set aside potentially overflowing cups. James Smith offered this helpful perspective:

> "We simply do not have enough time to do all that we would like to do. When we add too many things in our lives, something has to be eliminated. Unfortunately, busy people often rid themselves of the most important ones: relationships, spiritual practices and self-care."

Rather than choosing Martha's "many things," we want to learn how to experience Mary's "one" thing. Their story reminds us that saying no to desirable activity (like being a good hostess), is sometimes necessary so we can say yes to something better for our soul (like sitting with Jesus).

In what ways do you prioritize filling your internal cup over productivity and activity?

2. Create Margin in Our Days

Ken Gire is one of my favorite authors. In *The Reflective Life*, Gire reprinted a condensed chapter from another of his books. To squeeze an 11-page chapter into just a few pages, Gire reduced the font size.

He also removed the usual spacing between paragraphs, leaving each sentence to run into the next. Gire's first question at the end of this condensed chapter wasn't, *"What did you think?"* It was, *"At what point did you stop reading?"* His intent was to illustrate our need for margin not only on the printed page but also in our lives. **Identifying and focusing upon what's important becomes more difficult without margin in our days.** Yet as Nouwen observed, we instinctively push against carving out this space:

> "Being busy, active and on the move has nearly become part of our constitution. When we are asked to sit in a chair, without a paper to read, a radio to listen to, a television to watch, without a visitor or a phone, we are inclined to become so restless and tense that we welcome anything that will distract us again."

It's no coincidence that before describing an overflowing cup, the psalmist stated, "He makes me lie down in green pastures, he leads me beside still waters, he restores my soul" (Psalm 23:2-3). **To experience God's filling of our cup to overflowing, we must position ourselves to receive it.** A little over 10 years ago at a spiritual retreat for pastors led by Ruth Haley Barton, I rediscovered a life-giving practice that's helped me with this positioning. It was actually something that I had done many years earlier until . . . (wait for it) . . . busyness eventually crowded it from my routine.

Since that retreat, I try to create space within for God to fill my cup by sitting quietly in His presence for 20 minutes each morning. This isn't a time of activity, when I pray or read my Bible; my goal is to simply be present with the Lord during these moments—"practicing the presence of God," as Brother Lawrence put it. To be honest, I'm rarely aware of anything impactful that occurs during this time. But I trust that creating space in this way pleases the Lord the same way a parent enjoys a sleeping child on her lap, and that it's connecting us more closely together.

Robert Barron highlighted the importance of margin in our lives, stating, **"The deepest part of the soul likes to go slow, since it seeks to savor rather than to accomplish; it wants to rest in and contemplate the good rather than hurry off to another place."** Mary created this time for Jesus, even with busyness and noise around her, and we can do the same. If inactivity or spending time in silence feels too difficult to consider, let me gently suggest this may signal the need to do exactly that, even if just for five minutes each day.

How can you to create daily margin that allows your cup to be filled by God?

3. Cultivate Space Within

In Jesus' parable of the sower, a path was one of four locations where seed fell, and one of three where it didn't flourish. Paths by their very nature are packed hard, which is sometimes true of our internal spiritual soil. Without realizing it, constant activity and responsibilities can pack us tightly within. A tendency toward full days can create internal clutter, prompting Soren Kierkegaard to state, **"If I were a doctor and were asked for my advice, I should reply: Create silence."** Overflowing cups require internal space that allows us to remain aware of and responsive to the Holy Spirit's life-giving stirring.

When I was growing up, our family cultivated a large garden each year. My dad's annual spring roto-tilling of the soil is one of my most vivid memories of the labor we poured into this garden.

(Ok, it was mostly my parents who did the work, but watching them took a lot out of me.) Winter weather compacted the soil, leaving little space under the surface for our garden seed to grow. For this reason, my dad painstakingly loosened the soil with his machine before new seed was planted.

I find this a helpful illustration of our need to monitor and loosen the hardness of our spiritual soil under the surface. It took a roto-tiller to soften the earthen soil of our family garden; it takes silence and times of inactivity to soften us spiritually within. When that happens, we'll have greater receptivity to the life-giving seed that God plants within us—and greater potential for refilled cups. John Ortberg offered another description in *Soul Keeping* of what this looks like:

> "Our soul is like an inner stream of water, which gives strength, direction and harmony to every other element of our life. When that stream is as it should be, we are constantly refreshed and exuberant in all we do . . . and all else within us is enlivened and directed by that stream."

Archbishop Francis Fenelon wrote, **"God does not cease speaking, but the noise of the creatures without, and of our passion within, deafens us, and stops our hearing."** Before more recent advancements, many of us used to search for radio stations by turning a dial and listening carefully to pick out the desired frequency from among other stations. Creating space within enables us to tune our hearts and minds to the frequency of God's Spirit, hearing what He wants to say and receiving His filling of our cups. For this reason, the Lord instructed His people, "Be still and know that I am God" (Psalm 46:10).

In what ways can you regularly create space within?

Final Thought

Author Lettie Cowman wrote a century ago of a traveler who organized a long journey deep into the African jungle. The expedition went much farther than expected on the first day, causing the traveler to anticipate a quicker arrival at their destination. He was dismayed the next morning, therefore, to discover that local tribesmen hired to carry their equipment were sitting around camp, refusing to move. When the traveler angrily questioned their inactivity, he was informed that the group had gone so far and so fast on the first day, these locals were now waiting for their souls to catch up to their bodies.

We could learn much from these primitive tribesmen. Finishing well becomes easier when our soul is caught up to the rest of us and our cup is overflowing on a regular basis. As we learn to value internal health as much as external activity, we'll be positioned to say with the psalmist, "My cup overflows."

Chapter 12

DEVELOP A BIGGER PERSPECTIVE

My life is but a weaving between my God and me.
I cannot choose the colors He weaveth steadily.
'Oft times He weaveth sorrow; and I in foolish pride
Forget He sees the upper and I the underside.
Not 'til the loom is silent and the shuttles cease to fly
Will God unroll the canvas and reveal the reason why
The dark threads are as needful in the weaver's skillful hand
As the threads of gold and silver in the pattern He has
planned.
— Corrie ten Boom

A college senior signed up for a class on Introductory Bird Watching, after hearing that it was taught by an older professor who gave everyone at least a C grade. Unfortunately, the professor retired before the class began and was replaced by a young teacher who wanted to demonstrate his brilliance. The course became much more challenging than anticipated, and the last straw was the final exam. It consisted of 25 pair of bird legs from the knees down, with instructions to name each bird. Realizing he didn't know any of the answers, the senior angrily stood up, loudly crumpled up the exam, and threw it in the wastebasket on his way out the room.

Unhappy with this reaction, the teacher reached for his grade book and asked, "Young man, what is your name?"

The student rolled his pants up to his knees and replied, "You tell me!"

Identifying a bird by only its legs would be difficult for most of us. It's often just as hard to understand the bigger picture of God's activity when we only have incomplete glimpses to go on. **Finishing well becomes easier when we're able to trust that God is up to more than we can visibly see.** But this isn't always our natural inclination when life gets hard.

The wisdom of our years helps us weather challenges more easily than when we were younger; there's greater depth to our perspective, and we benefit from the backdrop of lessons learned along the way. Still, there are moments in life when we long to better understand what God is doing and how that intersects with our story. This desire for clarity often occurs during times of loss or challenge—experiences that become all too familiar as we age. Our range of physical capabilities and activity decrease over time, even as health issues multiply. Memory loss becomes a reality for some and an anxious threat for many more.

Places of deficiency often narrow our focus. What we don't have or what isn't going well becomes the lens through which we view our lives, especially when we're hurt, confused or overwhelmed. We instinctively assume that what we see is how things are, and it's difficult to believe there's more to our story than this. Such moments require more of our faith: we have to work harder to trust that God is acting for us in ways we cannot see. The Old Testament prophet Elijah's story provides a reassuring reminder that God is often up to more than we can glimpse.

Elijah's Story
One of my parenting failures occurred when Matthew was around

five years old and Suzanne around two. I took them with me one day to a computer store, where I wanted to look over some sale items. Shortly after we arrived, I discovered that Suzanne needed to use the bathroom. I still remember the moment when I was mentally congratulating myself for capably addressing my daughter's needs—and suddenly realized I'd forgotten to tell my son where we were going. Sure enough, we departed the bathroom to the sound of loud wailing from the front of the store. Quickly making my way there, I found Matthew in tears, believing that Suzanne and I had gone home and abandoned him at the store. The two store clerks trying to comfort my son looked relieved when I arrived, but a little doubtful of my parenting abilities when they handed him back to me.

Elijah was one of the Old Testament's greatest prophets, living during the ninth century B.C. Despite this prophet's bold faithfulness, our passage describes a time when he seemed to feel left on his own by God. Ironically, it immediately followed Elijah's dramatic victory over 450 false prophets. However, biblical stories don't always neatly conclude with happily-ever-after endings. They're real life accounts of people like us, who experience life's ups and downs and learn about God through both. Elijah's success quickly soured when Queen Jezebel responded by threatening his life—and the same man who stood his ground against hundreds suddenly fled at the threat of one:

> Elijah was afraid and ran for his life. When he came to Beersheba in Judah, he left his servant there, while he himself went a day's journey into the wilderness. He came to a broom bush, sat down under it and prayed that he might die. "I have had enough, LORD," he said. "Take my life; I am

no better than my ancestors." Then he lay down under the bush and fell asleep.

All at once an angel touched him and said, "Get up and eat." He looked around, and there by his head was some bread baked over hot coals, and a jar of water. He ate and drank and then lay down again.

The angel of the LORD came back a second time and touched him and said, "Get up and eat, for the journey is too much for you." So he got up and ate and drank. Strengthened by that food, he traveled forty days and forty nights until he reached Horeb, the mountain of God. There he went into a cave and spent the night.

And the word of the LORD came to him: "What are you doing here, Elijah?"

He replied, "I have been very zealous for the LORD God Almighty. The Israelites have rejected your covenant, torn down your altars, and put your prophets to death with the sword. I am the only one left, and now they are trying to kill me too."

The LORD said, "Go out and stand on the mountain in the presence of the LORD, for the LORD is about to pass by."

Then a great and powerful wind tore the mountains apart and shattered the rocks before the LORD, but the LORD was not in the wind. After the wind there was an earthquake, but the LORD was not in the earthquake. After the earthquake came a fire, but the LORD was not in the fire. And after the fire came a gentle whisper. When Elijah heard it, he pulled his cloak over his face and went out and stood at the mouth of the cave.

Then a voice said to him, "What are you doing here, Elijah?"

He replied, "I have been very zealous for the LORD God Almighty. The Israelites have rejected your covenant, torn down your altars, and put your prophets to death with the sword. I am the only one left, and now they are trying to kill me too."

The LORD said to him, "Go back the way you came, and go to the Desert of Damascus. When you get there, anoint Hazael king over Aram. Also, anoint Jehu son of Nimshi king over Israel, and anoint Elisha son of Shaphat from Abel Meholah to succeed you as prophet. Jehu will put to death any who escape the sword of Hazael, and Elisha will put to death any who escape the sword of Jehu. Yet I reserve seven thousand in Israel—all whose knees have not bowed down to Baal and whose mouths have not kissed him." (I Kings 19:3-18)

Throughout the Bible, God's followers frequently encountered resistance. Moses, Jeremiah, and Paul were among those whose faithfulness resulted in adversity; yet when it occurred, they and others stood strong. One early church leader named Chrysostom, when threatened with banishment by Queen Eudocia, simply responded, "Go, tell her I fear nothing but sin." In contrast to others who faithfully stood their ground, Elijah responded by fleeing. His prophetic role was of little use to God out in the wilderness. Elijah also set an uninspiring example for all who remained faithful to God, including those who had just destroyed Jezebel's prophets. But Elijah didn't care. All he could see was the immediacy of his needs, and what he lacked.

Elijah's places of deficiency were many. Feeling threatened by Jezebel, he "was afraid and ran for his life" (19:3). Elijah's emotional depletion prompted him to cry out in despair, "I have had enough, Lord. Take my life" (19:4). His physical exhaustion led him twice to "lay down" (19:5-6); he also "ate and drank" two times (19:6,8). Finally, Elijah's spiritual discouragement resulted in his repeated complaint, "I am the only one left" (19:10, 14). Any one of these challenges could easily knock us off balance. All of them together were overwhelming for Elijah.

Jewish philosopher Martin Buber made a telling observation about stories like Elijah's: "Whereas history, as the world writes it, glorifies success, the Bible glorifies those who have failed." That's because **God's redeeming work is often most clearly revealed in our failures.** Our familiarity with stories like Elijah's sometimes prevents us from appreciating how differently God could have responded. The Lord could have exhorted Elijah to get back into action; he could also have demanded greater faith or expressed disappointment with Elijah's retreat. Instead, God responded with patient, loving care. After providing for Elijah's needs and sending him on a 40-day journey *away* from the battle zone, God provided a lesson that not only enlarged Elijah's perspective, it changed him.

Elijah could only see what wasn't going well. Self-pity dripped from his Eeyore-like lament, "I'm the only one left." When God offered Elijah a second opportunity to change his tune, the prophet stuck to the same complaint. Forty days after experiencing God's patient and loving care, Elijah still despaired. His perspective remained defined by the lens of what he didn't have and what wasn't going well. Imagine Elijah's surprise when he learned how inaccurate his perception was. Elijah was *not* alone. God had preserved not 70 or even 700, but 7000 others who were also faithful to him. In that moment, Elijah discovered that God was up to far more than his narrow focus had allowed him to see.

The chapters following Elijah's encounter with God describe what Paul Harvey often referred to as *"The rest of the story."* Elijah's discovery that God was doing more than he had perceived dramatically transformed his actions and demeanor. In the following days, boldness and conviction replaced discouragement and self-pity. **Elijah's enlarged perspective changed his approach to life and to God and reveals what's possible for us.**

Our Story

The Manchester Guardian newspaper ran a television advertisement years ago, showing the same event from three different angles. In the first scene, a skinhead with tattoos and body piercings ran directly at a well-dressed businessman carrying a brief case, knocking him down. Viewers assumed they were observing a mugging, and that the skinhead slammed the man to the ground to rob him. A different angle for the second scene showed a car pulling up behind the skinhead. After three big men got out, the skinhead ran toward the businessman and knocked him down. With this view, it appeared that the skinhead was chased by plainclothes police officers and hit the man while trying to get away.

When the scene ran a third time, the angle was from above. It revealed a safe dangling precariously from a crane directly above the businessman, about to slip, fall, and crush him. Viewers immediately understood the true story: the skinhead noticed the danger and was sprinting to save the man's life while risking his own. The ad concluded by asserting that readers could count on *The Manchester Guardian* to provide the right perspective.

Elijah's discovery that God was doing more than he could see provides an encouraging example for us. When we struggle to recognize the Lord's involvement in our circumstances, we'll often respond like Elijah, believing there's little more to our story than what we perceive and how we interpret it. God's interaction with Elijah on Mount Horeb encourages us to develop a larger perspective than we sometimes possess. **We want to more easily look beyond trial, loss or deficiency and trust a bigger story of God's activity and leading in our lives than circumstances may suggest.** Let's explore two actions that can help move us toward this larger perspective.

1. Maintain Balance

Before enlarging Elijah's perspective, God helped him regain balance. The Lord allowed Elijah to get the sleep he obviously needed and restored him with food and drink. Though Elijah wasn't doing *what* God had called him to, the Lord demonstrated concern with *how* he was doing. His response to Elijah offers an encouraging glimpse of God's care for our well-being, even when we fall short of His desires. This is great news, for our frequent shortcomings often fuel a perception that God is constantly disappointed with us. The Lord's caring response to Elijah provides a revealing glimpse of the grace He extends to us.

Like Elijah, our perspective can become distorted when we're out of balance. I've learned that when I'm overly tired, small problems become big problems. We react in such moments like a group that was shown a sheet of white paper with a blot in the middle. When asked what they saw, every person mentioned the blot; not one acknowledged the white space that filled most of the page. Unfortunately, we're sometimes unable to see more than the blot we're currently dealing with, or to remember the bigger reality around it. That's when the input of a spouse or friends can be helpful. Their observation that we're making things bigger than they really are can be as helpful as a car's warning light that something's amiss.

Maintaining balance helps us grasp a fuller understanding of all our story, rather than seeing just a smaller portion of it. When needs or places of deficiency begin defining our view of life, this may be a signal that we're out of balance physically or emotionally in ways that distort our perspective. Our best response is to prioritize getting the sleep or space we need that enables us to regain our equilibrium. As we do, problems will more likely regain their rightful size; though still present, they'll hopefully seem more manageable.

How do you seek to regain balance when your perspective becomes distorted?

2. Look for God in the Picture

My first ministry position was leading a group of young single adults in Newport Beach, California. Shortly after arriving, I decided that offering a series on sexuality might attract more singles. But as the first Sunday approached, I became increasingly nervous about what I had advertised and was stepping into. More than 30 years later, I still remember sitting in worship before teaching the first lesson, wishing I was sick so I could go home and avoid it. No such luck—in fact, the morning's challenge increased. When I began teaching, the lectern I was leaning on collapsed. I then realized, partway thru my lesson, that I had inadvertently omitted one of my best illustrations. As I concluded, I felt I had just wasted peoples' morning. Embarrassed, I remember wanting to slip out of the room during my closing prayer, so I could avoid meeting their eyes after class.

Imagine my surprise, therefore, when someone approached me afterwards, asking if my lesson had been recorded. Then another person thanked me for what she said was one of the best talks she'd heard on that topic. I learned a powerful lesson that morning: God was doing something I would have missed without the input of these individuals. As I discovered, the Lord will sometimes use others to help us glimpse His presence and activity that we might otherwise miss. On other occasions He'll directly expand our understanding, as the Holy Spirit reveals new insights and ways of seeing things. I recently experienced this perspective-enlarging in another way.

Near the end of a two-week period when I was at church during the day or on call at night for all but one of those days, I was discouraged by how these constant responsibilities were wearing me down. Then the Lord gently reminded me of the relaxing vacation I had taken just the previous month, when I sought to rest well before this demanding period that I knew was coming. This larger perspective immediately altered my perception of my experience. Circumstances hadn't changed, but my view of them became different. Weariness was replaced with gratitude for the Lord's restful provision that prepared me for these demands. Seeing God in the picture reshaped how I interpreted my story and helped my challenge assume its rightful size.

Passenger side windows in today's cars include the warning, "Objects in mirror are closer than they appear." Something similar can be true when it comes to our view of life. When we allow places of loss or challenge to dominate our perspective, they can loom larger than they actually are. Such moments cause us to forget that God is closer than it appears. That's why it's always important to look for a bigger picture that includes the Lord.

Elijah mentored a prophet named Elisha, who eventually succeeded him. On one occasion, when Elisha's servant was discouraged by soldiers surrounding their city, "Elisha prayed, 'O Lord, open his eyes so he may see.' Then the Lord opened the servant's eyes, and he looked and saw the hills full of horses and chariots of fire all around Elisha" (II Kings 6:17). Asking God to open our eyes so we can better see what He's up to can do wonders in restoring challenges to their rightful size.

Elijah was one of the Bible's greatest prophets, but the lesson he needed from God on Mount Horeb reveals how easily we can develop a too-small narrative of our lives. As a result of his enlarged perspective, Elijah boldly moved forward with renewed confidence. Fortunately, we don't have to make a 40-day journey to a mountain to learn this; we can ask God to enlarge our perspective each day right where we are.

What helps you see God in the bigger picture of your story?

<u>**Final Thought**</u>
Pastor Barbara Brown Taylor offered an example of our challenge to recognize and interpret God's activity in our lives:

> "Several summers ago I spent three days on a barrier island where loggerhead turtles were laying their eggs. One night while the tide was out, I watched a huge female heave herself up the beach to dig her nest and empty herself into it. Afraid of disturbing her, I left before she had finished her work but returned next morning to see if I could find the spot where her eggs lay hidden in the sand. What I found were her tracks, only they led in the wrong direction. Instead of heading back out to sea, she had wandered into the dunes, which were already hot as asphalt in the morning sun.

A little ways inland I found her, exhausted and all but baked, her head and flippers caked with dried sand. After pouring water on her, I fetched a park ranger who returned with a jeep to rescue her. As I watched in horror, he flipped her over on her back, wrapped tire chains around her front legs, and hooked the chains to the trailer hitch on his jeep. Then he took off, yanking her body forward so fast that her open mouth filled with sand and then disappeared underneath her as her neck bent so far I feared it would break.

The ranger hauled her over the dunes and down onto the beach; I followed the path that the prow of her shell cut in the sand. At ocean's edge, he unhooked her and turned her right side up again. She lay motionless in the surf as the water lapped at her body, washing the sand from her eyes and making her skin shine again. Then a particularly large wave broke over her and she lifted her head slightly, moving her back legs as she did. As I watched, she revived. Every fresh wave brought her life back to her until one of them made her light enough to find a foothold and push off, back into water that was her home."

Then Taylor concluded with this observation about the challenge of accurate perceptions:

"Watching her swim slowly away and remembering her nightmare ride through the dunes, I noted that it is sometimes hard to tell whether you are being killed or saved by the hands that turn your life upside down."

In moments of discouragement or confusion, let's remember that

God is often doing more than we may recognize. Developing a larger perspective that better sees His presence and activity in the picture will enhance our confident continuation toward finishing well.

PART IV
LOOKING AHEAD

Chapter 13

PROPELLED FORWARD BY HOPE

"Hope isn't merely a nice option that helps us temporarily clear a hurdle. It's essential to our survival."

— Chuck Swindoll

In 1981, Eugene Lang stood to deliver a commencement address to 61 sixth-graders graduating from Public School 121 in East Harlem. Lang had attended the school more than 50 years earlier, before going on to achieve a successful business career. He planned to encourage these students that they could do the same—but as he stood before them, Lang realized his words would fall short. Recent history suggested that many of these sixth-graders would eventually drop out of school. Abruptly abandoning his speech, Lang instead impulsively offered a scholarship to any student eventually admitted to a four-year college. Lang promised to put $2,000 aside towards college for each student and add to that amount every year they remained in school.

Following Lang's speech, the school's principle predicted to him that one or two students might take advantage of his offer. Amazingly, half of that sixth-grade class eventually enrolled in public or private college, and nearly 90% graduated from high school. As one student explained, "I had something to look forward to, something waiting for me."

The importance of something to look forward to cannot be over-emphasized. Finishing well involves looking ahead with hope, trusting that experiences still before us are worth moving toward. Scottish pastor Thomas Chalmers identified what he considered three grand essentials for happiness: *something to do, something to love,* and *something to hope for.* While the first two qualities are rooted in the present, the third finds meaning in the future. Hope is like the proverbial carrot out in front that motivates us to continue moving forward. Victor Frankl described hope's importance in *Man's Search for Meaning,* asserting, "**It is a peculiarity of man that he can only live by looking to the future.**"

Hope of future good enables us to rise above present challenges. When a medical diagnosis wasn't what we expected, hope of beating it carries us through the treatments. When a spouse or close friend dies and we're not sure we can continue without their presence, hope gives us strength to face another day. When physical limitations slow us down, hope points us toward meaningful activity that still engages us. When difficult experiences threaten to overwhelm us, hope in God's assistance keeps us clinging to Him. Years ago, I saw a greeting card (obviously dated) that read, *Wouldn't it be nice if life was like a VCR, and we could fast forward through the tough times?* Though we lack this fast-forwarding ability, hope can carry us through even the toughest of times.

During my seminary years, Lewis Smedes was one of my favorite professors. He noted in *Keeping Hope Alive,* "**Our spirits were made for hope the way our hearts were made to love and our brains were made to think and our hands were made to make things.**" The author of Hebrews aptly described hope as "an anchor for the soul" (Hebrews 6:19). Our next story of Habakkuk powerfully models how hope of what lies ahead can keep us moving forward, even when everything around us is bleak.

Habakkuk's Story

The Bible usually provides some background information about Old Testament prophets, such as their family, prior occupation or hometown. But we're told nothing of Habakkuk; the best we can surmise is that he lived in Jerusalem when his words were recorded. Habakkuk's prophetic role occurred late in the seventh century B.C., when Babylon had emerged as the new dominant power. After Babylon defeated the Egyptians and Assyrians, Habakkuk was concerned about the threat that it posed to the Southern Kingdom of Judah. Additionally, the unfaithfulness of God's people had resulted in spiritual and moral decay that dismayed Habakkuk. His contribution is unusual among the 12 Minor Prophet Old Testament books, for he spoke no words of exhortation or warning to a nation. Instead, the prophet's words were directed to God, resulting in the Lord's patient responses. Their dialogue provides an encouraging reminder of God's willingness to engage us even when we question His ways.

Habakkuk, obviously unhappy with God's lack of involvement in the circumstances of His people, began with a complaint:

> How long, O Lord, must I call for help, but you do not listen? Or cry out to you, "Violence!" but you do not save? Why do you make me look at injustice? Why do you tolerate wrong?" (Habakkuk 1:2-3)

Habakkuk's description of violence, injustice, and wrong-doing suggests that things were bleak wherever he turned. The wicked were having their way, and the prophet saw no intervention from God. In his frustration, Habakkuk went directly to the Lord, rather than complain *about* God's seeming indifference or turn away from Him. Like the psalmists, he grabbed hold of God and cried out for answers.

Habakkuk's complaint led to a response from God—but it wasn't one that eased the prophet's mind. The Lord assured Habakkuk of His coming intervention but stated that it would favor the Babylonians over His people. Because Babylon was a pagan nation, it must have shaken Habakkuk to learn that God would take *its* side. The Babylonians had a reputation for ruthlessness, and God acknowledged that they were "feared and dreaded," with a "bent on violence" (Habakkuk 1:7, 9). Why would the Lord allow them to prevail over His people? Though God had repeatedly warned the Israelites about their lack of faithfulness, nothing had changed. The Lord understood that it would take something drastic like a Babylonian conquest to get their attention and re-orient their hearts toward Him.

In His response, God said something else to Habakkuk:

"I am going to do something in your days that you would not believe, even if you were told" (Habakkuk 1:5).

Habakkuk had asked, "Why don't you do something?" When the Lord responded that He would, He went on to explain, "Even if I told you what I'm doing, you won't understand." God knew His people were about to experience difficult times, and that His purposes couldn't be easily grasped. After a second series of complaints from Habakkuk, the Lord returned to this message, informing the prophet that only in God's "appointed time" (Habakkuk 2:3) would things become clear. These words remind us that the Lord's purposes often aren't as obvious on the front end of events as we'd like. As a result, we're left to hope and trust that in God's good timing, we'll eventually understand how He's working for our good.

This dialogue during the first two chapters sets the stage for Habakkuk's final response in chapter 3. This prophet who had been peppering God with difficult questions about His seeming inactivity abruptly turned to praise. Shifting from complaint to prayer, Habakkuk's closing words offer one of the Bible's most beautiful expressions of hope. The prophet expressed trust in and even praise for God's activity, even when he saw nothing to reinforce it:

"Though the fig tree does not bud
 and there are no grapes on the vines,
though the olive crop fails
 and the fields produce no food,
though there are no sheep in the pen
 and no cattle in the stalls,
yet I will rejoice in the LORD,
 I will be joyful in God my Savior.

The Sovereign LORD is my strength;
 he makes my feet like the feet of a deer,
 he enables me to tread on the heights." (Habakkuk 3:17-19)

Habakkuk still couldn't understand what the Lord was doing, nothing around him had improved, and things were about to become worse. Despite all this, he placed his trust in God. Habakkuk resolved to rejoice in God's goodness, even when life around him offered little reason for doing so. Only hope could prompt such a remarkable response. This hope enabled Habakkuk to move forward in confidence—if not in his circumstances, then at least in his God. **Habakkuk's response demonstrates the power of hope's light when all around us is dark.** Similar words were written during World War II on a cellar wall in Cologne, Germany by Jews hiding from Nazis:

> *I believe in the sun even when it is not shining.*
> *I believe in love even when feeling it not.*
> *I believe in God even when He is silent.*

Our Story

When I moved from Washington at the age of 25 to attend seminary in Pasadena, California, I left behind everything I knew: friends, church, family, job—and a state I'd lived in my entire life. After taking a few classes at Fuller Seminary's Seattle extension for two years, I decided to study full-time at the main campus. I planned to earn a PhD that would enable me to pursue ministry with college students like my mentor Ed.

After arriving in early July, my first summer class was more challenging than any I'd previously taken. As a result, I realized after a week that while I could probably earn a PhD, I wouldn't enjoy the process and needed to let that plan go. Suddenly, I had no idea what I was doing in this new and unfamiliar environment, or what my next steps should be. I wondered if this meant that I should move back home. If I stayed, I had no clue what classes I should take during fall registration the following month. I urgently prayed to God each day, longing for wisdom to discern my next steps.

After weeks of uncertainty, God responded one morning in the clearest way I've ever experienced. While praying for guidance, I suddenly heard the Lord say to me as if someone audibly spoke the words: *You're where I want you to be.* That was it—but it was enough.

Though this response offered no clarity about my future, it provided the encouragement and confidence I needed to continue forward, trusting that my next steps would eventually become clear. More important, these words gave me hope. Despite moving to seminary for a reason that no longer applied, there was still some yet-to-be-discovered purpose to being there. A pastor friend eventually suggested that I keep my options open by working toward a Master of Divinity degree, and I happily did so because I enjoyed the learning. Years later, that was the degree I needed to become a pastor when I sensed the Lord's call to ministry.

During subsequent years, I've taught countless lessons and preached many sermons. Each began with the same two things (as did this book): a blank piece of paper and hope that the Lord would bring forth something out of nothing. Without this hope, I'm not sure I would have the courage to begin this process each time. Smedes explained, "Hope is the Creator's implant into us, his traveling children, on the move into a future we can imagine but cannot control. Hope is our fuel for the journey. **As long as we keep hope alive, we keep moving. To stop moving is to die of hope deficiency.**"

Chalmer's third grand essential may be the most important, for without hope, what we do and how we love may feel lacking. In the same way that hard hats and athletic helmets protect our head, hope protects us within. The tragic act of suicide is often prompted by a lack of hope for what lies ahead. Swindoll underscored hope's importance:

> "Take from us our wealth and we are hindered. Take our health and we are handicapped. Take our purpose and we are slowed, temporarily confused. But take away our hope

and we are plunged into deepest darkness . . . stopped dead in our tracks, paralyzed."

A nineteenth-century Portuguese sailing ship once ran out of water off the coast of South America. The crew and passengers suffered for many days, until eventually another ship approached. The Portuguese ship sent a message describing their problem and requesting assistance. The other ship responded simply, "Lower your buckets." It turns out the Portuguese ship was floating at the ninety-mile-wide mouth of the Amazon River, the largest river in the world, and was surrounded by freshwater.

Though God's love and provision give us reason to hope, that doesn't mean we'll automatically experience it. Hope also requires something of us: we must lower our bucket into the hope-filled waters of our Lord's assurances. Two approaches can help us develop a deep reservoir of hope that propels us forward, like Habakkuk, through circumstances that sometimes offer little reason for hope.

1. Establish a Sure Foundation

In one of His parables, Jesus encouraged His followers to build their faith upon a foundation that would hold them up when storms occurred (Matthew 7:24-27). Hope requires a similar sure foundation that will hold us up and keep us moving us forward when we're buffeted by life. Many place their hope in external possibilities that can too easily disappoint or fade with time: a significant relationship, a sizeable nest-egg, or a fun-filled life. In contrast, the Christian faith offers a hope foundation that's unchanging and substantial. We hope in the goodness and power of God to do what we cannot. Eugene Peterson noted:

"What we call hoping is often only wishing. We want things we think are impossible, but we have better sense than to spend any money or commit our lives to them. **Biblical hope, though . . . acts on the conviction that God will complete the work that he has begun even when the appearances, especially when the appearances, oppose it.**"

Admittedly, much of what we hope for won't be faith-based. However, a deep foundation built upon hoping in our Lord can hold us up when other hopes don't come to fruition. What contributes to such a foundation? First, we hope in *God's redeeming power.* My wonderful ministry mentor, Bill Flanagan, once described a sign in a storefront that read, *"No chair so broken that it cannot be repaired."* He went on to suggest that we insert the word "life" for "chair." The same power that triumphed over sin and death through Christ's resurrection is available to us. When our days seem dark and our options limited, God can turn things around.

Second, we hope in *God's constant presence.* Troubles can sometimes seem greater when we face them alone. Christ's promise to His disciples, "I am with you always" (Matthew 28:20), assures us that He accompanies us through all that we encounter. Our Lord's personal presence, experienced through the Holy Spirit, can strengthen us within. As John Ortberg stated, "Faith is not simply holding beliefs. At its core, faith . . . puts trust in a person."

Third, we hope in *God's sovereignty over this world.* It's increasingly easy to become discouraged by division and darkness that fills our world. Our hope rests in understanding that this is God's world, and that He cares about it even more than we do. The Lord will ultimately prevail in restoring His creation and His loved ones who live in it. Jesus assured us, "In this world you will have trouble. But take heart! I have overcome the world" (John 16:33).

Finally, we hope in *God's eternal assurances*. Paul promises, "No eye has seen, no ear has heard, no mind has conceived what God has prepared for those who love Him" (I Corinthians 2:9). When present circumstances seem bleak, we find hope in the Lord's assurance of a better future. One day, good will prevail, all will make sense, and we'll enjoy a fullness of life beyond anything that we've yet experienced.

These sources of hope all require faith, so it's fitting that the Bible repeatedly links hope with faith. Faith and hope are often synonymous throughout the Old Testament. In the New Testament, Hebrews 11:1 declared, *"Faith* is confidence in what we *hope* for." Paul's beautiful exposition on love identified *faith, hope* and love as the greatest qualities (I Corinthians 13:13). Paul also connected these three in his letter to the Thessalonians (I Thessalonians 1:3). Brazilian theologian Rubem Alvez beautifully described the interplay between faith and hope: "**Hope is hearing the music of the future. Faith is dancing to it**" in the present.

That brings to mind my practice of listening to music on my phone when I fly. At some point during the flight, I'll inevitably hear a song in my earphones that causes my head to nod and feet to tap in rhythm. I'm caught up in a tune no one around me can hear, that isn't reflected in my surrounding environment. Our relationship with God similarly provides notes of hope; in faith, we hum and tap our feet to them as we move through life. During inevitable disconnects between where we are and where we want to be, hope in what God can yet do stands in the gap, providing fuel for our faith. Smedes declared:

"Hope comes alive with the birth of faith and stays alive as

long as we keep believing. We hope only for what we believe is possible. No matter what we put our faith in, we will sing the song of hope only to the tune of faith. **Hope, we could say, is faith with an eye to the future."**
What helps form your foundation of hope?

2. Identify Realistic and Meaningful Hopes

I enjoyed writing during high school, and was Sports Editor, then Editor of our school newspaper. I continued as Sports Editor of my college newspaper my first two years, then interned at *National Journal* magazine in Washington, D.C. during my junior year. I briefly hoped for a career in writing after college, until realizing that I had little to say as a 22-year-old. After setting aside that desire, I've occasionally thought over the years that I might pick it back up again during retirement.

Four years ago, I was the retreat speaker for a delightful group of Christian Missionary and Alliance retired missionaries. Their response was gracious and encouraging, but one comment stood out. During breakfast our final morning, a participant casually encouraged me to write a book on what I'd taught that week. Something instantly leapt within me at these words, and I realized it was time to reconsider this activity I'd put aside more than 35 years earlier.

The writing process behind this book has been much more difficult the past two years than I had expected—certainly harder than preparing a sermon or lesson. There's something about the written word remaining on a page that makes me want to get it just right. As a result, I've spent many, many more hours on this labor of love than I would prefer to count. What's continued propelling me forward, willing to spend yet another portion of a day on a chapter re-write, is the hope that these thoughts might encourage others.

If hope is to sustain us along our journey of finishing well, it must be big and clear enough to propel us forward, especially during difficult times. Many of the hopes that fill our days are of a smaller nature. Growing up, we hoped the teacher wouldn't call on us, or that someone we liked might like us back. As young adults, we hoped to get to work on time during difficult mornings, or to save enough money for a vacation. Later in life, we hope we'll make it to retirement, or that a knee replacement will improve our quality of life. Obviously, we also have much bigger hopes than these along the way—and it's these hopes that we need to nurture and remain aware of.

I read of someone who said, "*My goal is to live forever. So far, so good.*" Sounds good—for now. But it's not a winning approach to a lasting hope that's meaningful. Our hopes need to be clear enough that we can keep them in sight. They need to be realistic enough that we know they're possible. And they need to be big enough and feel important enough that they'll keep us moving forward. Here are a few:

- We hope that we'll become a better person than we are today;
- We hope for the well-being of our loved ones;
- We hope that our days will be filled with meaningful activity;
- We hope that tomorrow will be as good as—if not better than—today.

I'm hesitant to add one more quote from Smedes—but as I mentioned earlier, he *was* one of my favorite seminary professors. Smedes noted the importance of clear and compelling hopes, writing,

> "We need to know what we hope for because our hopes are too important to leave in a jumbled heap like a basket of unsorted laundry. . . We all tend to become what we most hope for, so

taking inventory of our hopes is a way of taking inventory of our future selves."

What are 2-3 things that you most hope for?

Final Thought
Chuck Swindoll described the importance of hope:

When we are trapped in a tunnel of misery, hope points to the light at the end.

When we are overworked and exhausted, hope gives us fresh energy.

When we are discouraged, hope lifts our spirits.

When we are tempted to quit, hope keeps us going.

When we lose our way and confusion blurs the destination, hope dulls the edge of panic.

When we struggle with a crippling disease or a lingering illness, hope helps us persevere beyond the pain.

When we fear the worst, hope brings reminders that God is still in control.

When we must endure the consequences of bad decisions, hope fuels our recovery.

When we find ourselves unemployed, hope tells us that we still have a future.

When we are forced to sit back and wait, hope gives us the patience to trust.

When we feel rejected and abandoned, hope reminds us we're not alone . . . we'll make it.

When we say our final farewell to someone we love, hope in the life beyond gets us through our grief.

Paul recognized the importance of hope when he wrote, "**May the God of hope fill you with all joy and peace as you trust in him, so that you may overflow with hope by the power of the Holy Spirit**" (Romans 15:13). As you continue forward along your journey of finishing well, don't overlook the powerful role that hope plays in propelling you forward.

Chapter 14

MOVE FORWARD WITH COURAGE

"Old age ain't no place for sissies."
—Bette Davis

A medicine man sat at a fork in the road deep in the jungle. An approaching traveler watched him continuously toss a stick in the air and closely watch how it landed. When the traveler eventually asked the medicine man what he was doing, he replied, "I am asking the medicine stick which way I am to go. As it falls to the ground it points the way."

The traveler continued, "And why do you throw it so many times?"

"Because I don't want to go where the stick is pointing!" came the response.

When we think of finishing well, we envision a path of our choosing: our health will remain good, we'll live out the years ahead in a familiar home, and we'll share them with those most important to us. But **finishing well often requires making the best of life when it veers in directions not of our choosing, and we don't know what lies ahead**. These unexpected turns tend to occur more often than we may anticipate.

When I recently attended a retirement seminar, the speaker encouraged us to think of all the change that occurred in our lives from age 20 to 50. He then noted that we'll likely experience just as much change between age 65 to 95. His point was to anticipate lots of change during our later years, rather than become surprised when it occurs. Finishing well, therefore, includes adapting to unexpected and unfamiliar changes while continuing to confidently move forward. We don't allow uncertainty of what lies ahead to dampen our spirit.

As our church's Pastor of Caring Ministry, some of my most meaningful ministry interactions are with those near the end of life. Because of these experiences, I've pondered more frequently than most in their fifties what the end of my own journey might be like. I confess that I sometimes cringe at the thought of those years, after witnessing many less than ideal situations. But as Mark Twain noted, "Do not complain about growing old. It is a privilege denied to many."

I recently had lunch with a friend in his late 70s who has lost much of his energy in recent years and is now caring for his homebound wife. He poignantly shared during that conversation, "I didn't think my later years would look like this." We'll inevitably encounter unexpected challenges ahead that will be outside our control. What we *can* control is our response to these experiences, and our approach to the path that lies ahead. Just as God led many throughout the Bible into new experiences and opportunities, He'll lovingly and gently lead us forward into new chapters before us.

Our exploration of finishing well began with a story of Joshua when he was "very old." We'll conclude by looking at an earlier time in Joshua's life, at the outset of the book named after him.

Joshua's Story

The book of Joshua opened during a time of great change and uncertainty for the Israelites. Camped at the Jordan River as they waited to enter the Promised Land, their side of the river represented their life journey and all that was familiar to them. On the other side of the river was an unknown new land that God was inviting them into. The land's possibilities were offset by the challenges of change and new experiences that would stretch them. The Israelites were poised to move forward, but perhaps understandably uncertain how they would handle all that was unfamiliar before them.

God understands how uncertainty can result in hesitation, and provided reassurance to Joshua:

> After the death of Moses the servant of the LORD, the LORD said to Joshua son of Nun, Moses' aide: "Moses my servant is dead. Now then, you and all these people, get ready to cross the Jordan River into the land I am about to give to them—to the Israelites. I will give you every place where you set your foot, as I promised Moses. Your territory will extend from the desert to Lebanon, and from the great river, the Euphrates—all the Hittite country—to the Mediterranean Sea in the west. No one will be able to stand against you all the days of your life. As I was with Moses, so I will be with you; I will never leave you nor forsake you. Be strong and courageous, because you will lead these people to inherit the land I swore to their ancestors to give them.
>
> "Be strong and very courageous. Be careful to obey all the law my servant Moses gave you; do not turn from it to the right or to the left, that you may be successful wherever you go. Keep this Book of the Law always on your lips; meditate on it day and night, so that you may be careful to do everything written in it. Then you will be prosperous and successful. Have I not commanded

you? Be strong and courageous. Do not be afraid; do not be discouraged, for the LORD your God will be with you wherever you go." (Joshua 1:1-9)

The Lord began by acknowledging the past: "Moses my servant is dead" (Joshua 1:2). The previous book of Deuteronomy ended with the death of Israel's only leader since their escape from Egypt. The book of Joshua opened with a first for everyone on the riverbank: Moses wasn't there to lead them. When major life transitions occur, it's natural to feel the loss of previously familiar seasons, as well as uncertainty about what lies ahead. Israel was preparing for a new experience in a new land, with a new leader. Surely more than a few Israelites wished they were still back in the good old days, with Moses leading them forward.

Joshua felt the loss of Moses more than anyone. He had been Moses' aide, groomed over the years for this new role that he now assumed. Moses had undoubtedly been a father figure and mentor to Joshua during all their years together. When two people share as much life as these men, one's absence inevitably creates a huge hole for the other.

When we experience significant loss, we need to acknowledge what we've lost and give ourselves time to heal. But we can't live there forever. Understanding the significance of Moses' death for Joshua and the Israelites, the Lord instructed them to spend 30 days in mourning. Once that period ended, it was time to move forward. After acknowledging Moses' death, God instructed Joshua and the people to move into the next chapter of their lives. However, He didn't push them forward with tough love, leaving them to figure things out on their own. As Joshua began his new leadership role and the nation prepared for a new land, the Lord offered multiple assurances.

First, God offered a *promise* that could compel the Israelites forward from known into unknown: "I will give you every place where you set your foot" (Joshua 1:3). In the next verse, God described boundaries of their new home that stretched far beyond what they could see. It was an incredible promise for people who had never possessed their own land. As is often true of God's promises, it described a reality beyond what Joshua and the Israelites could see.

God next assured Joshua and the Israelites of his *power*: "No one will be able to stand against you all the days of your life" (Joshua 1:5a). Israel was about to kick in the front door of formidable inhabitants. It was commonly believed that no one could defeat the Anakites, who lived there. This probably contributed to the fear of 10 of Moses' spies 40 years earlier, who insisted that the danger they'd seen in the land was greater than what they could overcome even in God's power. Israel's years as desert nomads also compounded their challenge, for it prevented them from developing much experience in battle. God's encouragement looked beyond what these people had to offer to what He could provide—and the Lord's resources significantly changed the equation for what was to come.

God then assured Joshua and the Israelites of His *presence*: "As I was with Moses, so I will be with you; I will never leave you nor forsake you" (Joshua 1:5b). As the Israelites moved forward into the intimidating and unknown, they didn't do so alone. The same God who led the Israelites out of Egypt, provided water and manna in the desert, and kept them safe in a new and unfamiliar land for 40 years would continue accompanying them throughout their next chapter. During the following years, He did exactly that.

God's encouragement to Joshua during this challenging new

experience encourages us to confidently move forward into new and unfamiliar stretches along our life journey.

Our Story

As our kids were growing up, I loved planning our family vacations (and still do). These times together were among my highlights of the year, when I could step back from ministry demands that diluted my presence at home and focus solely upon Deborah, Matthew and Suzanne. I still have precious memories of many of these trips and experiences that we shared together—but one vacation was harder than the others.

A little more than 10 years ago, our family took a 10-day trip one summer when Matthew was nearly 16 and Suzanne 13. Near the end of that time, I suddenly realized family dynamics had changed, and that our vacations together would no longer be the same. Because swimming pools had provided fun family experiences over the years, I had booked a nice hotel with a river pool and wave pool for our last two nights away from home. However, this time was different; after a few minutes in the pool, both kids were done. I eventually learned that they were missing their friends and wished they could head home sooner to be with them.

I did two things that day. First, I purchased internet access from the hotel so Matthew and Suzanne could interact with friends at home through their social media connections. Then I found a quiet place in a corner by the swimming pool and privately shed some tears over the loss of family vacations that I understood wouldn't be the same again. While we've rarely recaptured the same family vacation dynamics, I've since enjoyed meaningful trips with each child individually, wonderful travel experiences with Deborah, and have now added a daughter-in-law (and a "grand-dog").

Each of us experience moments of change that require us to leave behind familiar and treasured experiences on our side of the river of life and move into new experiences on the other side. God's encouraging words to Joshua reveal four steps that can guide our approach to these moments.

1. Look Forward

Jeanne Calment was the world's oldest person whose age could be verified, living to 122. On her 120th birthday, Calment was asked to describe her vision for the future. Her reply: *"Very brief!"* That's a logical answer for someone 120 years old, but not for the rest of us who may have many years still ahead. God's first instruction to Joshua and the Israelites was to shift their gaze from the past (Moses) to the future (Promised Land). His words addressed an inclination to linger on the familiar past, rather than looking ahead to new experiences the Lord has for us on the other side of the river.

A car's viewing options provide an example of where our focus should be. Across the front stretches a large windshield that allows us to see everything out ahead. A rear-view mirror provides an opportunity to see what's behind us—but the size difference between it and the windshield reveals where our primary focus should be. Nostalgia about the past can be enjoyable, but we don't want to dwell so much upon years behind us that we give little thought to what still lies ahead. Former President John F. Kennedy noted, **"Those who look only to the past or present are certain to miss the future."** A friend in his eighties understands this, prominently displaying a sign in his home that declares, *"THESE are the good old days!"*

What would you say is your vision for your years ahead?

2. Rest in God's Promises

The Lord sought to strengthen Joshua with His promises about crossing the Jordan River; He does the same for us through other biblical promises. God's promises can reassure and hold us fast when the terrain begins to change around us. With this in mind, note three things that we learn from God's promise to Joshua.

First, *God remembered His promise.* When the Lord led the Israelites into the Promised Land, He finally fulfilled His centuries-old promise to Abraham. Many had surely wondered over the years whether this promise would ever come to fruition. Yet the Lord never forgot His promise, making good on it hundreds of years later when the time was right. He did the same with Jesus' arrival in our world, centuries after prophecies about a Savior. The longer we wait to experience God's promises, the less certain we may become about them. But just because God's promises are sometimes slow in coming doesn't mean that they're not on the way. **God always remembers what He promised and is actively working to fulfill it,** even when we can't glimpse any indication of His follow through.

Second, *nothing in God's promise suggested that things would be easy.* God commanded Joshua three times, "Be strong and courageous" (Joshua 1:6, 7, 9), including one "very courageous." The Lord knew His promise would lead to challenging situations when the Israelites felt inadequate and fearful. That's why he also instructed, "Do not be terrified; do not be discouraged" (Joshua 1:9). Though God has good things ahead for us, that doesn't mean our experience of them will always be easy. David Beck noted, "Discernment is hearing God say, 'Go this way.' But if he were to tell us what lay ahead, a lot of us would refuse to follow."

Finally, *the Israelites experienced God's promise only after they stepped out in faith.* Before they could live into what He had for them, they had to first cross the Jordan River. God's promises will often require us to take initial steps of faith in the direction He's leading, trusting that doing so will result in experiencing what He's promised. As Frederick Buechner put it, **"Faith is not being sure where you're going, but going anyway."**

Which of God's promises are most meaningful for you?

3. Remain Connected to God's Power

There's a joke about a guy who bought a chainsaw, then returned it two weeks later. He complained to the salesperson, "When I purchased this chainsaw, you assured me that it could cut down 50 trees an hour; I can only cut down two."

The salesperson offered to see what the problem was and started up the chainsaw. When he did, the guy jumped back in surprise, saying, "What's that noise?!"

God's assurance of power for Joshua and the Israelites also applies to us. When we feel inadequate about new paths before us, the Lord offers His resources in leading us along them. But just as an electric lamp only works when plugged into its power source, we must remain closely connected to God to experience His power. Israel learned this the hard way shortly after crossing the Jordan. Not realizing that a disconnect with God had developed because of sin in their midst, they headed into battle confident of another victory. Instead, they were routed because the Lord wasn't with them that day.

Many of us tend to skip the manufacturer's instructions when assembling an item or using it for the first time (or maybe it's just me). As we move forward into our new future, reading God's operating instructions (the Bible) helps us understand the power that He makes available to us. Time in prayer and a willingness to follow the Holy Spirit's leading keeps us connected to this power source.

In what ways do you remain connected with God?

4. One Step at a Time

Conquering a new land had to feel daunting for the Israelites; however, they didn't do it in a month or even a year. It took a long time to eventually settle into a land of their own. God previously told the Israelites that this was for their own good, saying, "The Lord your God will drive out those nations before you, little by little. You will not be allowed to eliminate them all at once, or the wild animals will multiply around you" (Deuteronomy 7:22). Their first step across the Jordan River was the start of significant movement forward. The same is true as we encounter new and uncertain experiences along our path of finishing well. Rather than worrying or wondering about the end result, we just need to take the first step, trusting that it will create momentum for others that follow.

An amusing example of this was provided by Frenchman Michel Lotito, who set a Guinness World Record. What did Lotito do to achieve that record? He ate an entire bicycle, tires and all! The key is that Lotito didn't eat it all at once. Over 17 days, between March 17 and April 2, 1977, he melted every portion of the bicycle into small, swallow able units, then ate each piece. Personally, I'd look for other ways to set a world record. But when it comes to finishing well, we don't need to have everything figured out on the front end. We just need to keep moving forward the best we can, day by day, step by step—even bite by bite.

What's one step forward that you sense God inviting you to take toward finishing well?

Final Thought

An unknown author offered another bicycle illustration with *The Road of Life*, describing traveling the journey ahead with our Lord:

When I met Christ, it seemed as though life was rather like a bike ride. But it was a tandem bike and I noticed Christ was in the back helping me pedal.

I don't know just when it was that he suggested we change places, but life has not been the same since.

When I had control, I knew the way. It was rather boring but predictable. It was the shortest distance between two points.

But when he took the lead he knew delightful long cuts up mountains and through rocky places at breakneck speeds. It was all I could do to hang on! Even though it looked like madness, he said "Pedal."

I worried and was anxious and asked, "Where are you taking me?" He laughed and didn't answer, and I started to learn to trust.

I forgot my boring life and entered into the adventure. When I'd say, "I'm scared," he'd lean back and touch my hand.

I did not trust him at first to be in control of my life. I thought he'd wreck it, but he knows bike secrets. He knew how to make it bend to take sharp corners, how to jump to clear high rocks and how to fly to shorten scary passages.

And I'm learning to shut up and pedal in the strangest places. I'm beginning to enjoy the view and cool breezes on my face with my delightful constant companion, Jesus Christ. And when I'm sure I just can't do it anymore, he just smiles and says, "Pedal."

Finishing well is as important to our Lord as it is to us. God invites us to follow Him forward into what He has next for us—and to understand that even when we're unsure where the path is heading, we can trust the one who leads us on it.

Author Biography

John Goodale serves as Pastor of Caring Ministries at First Presbyterian Church, Colorado Springs, where he has ministered for 25
years. John has been in ordained ministry for 30 years, and particularly enjoys working with the older membership of his church.

John and his wife Deborah have been married for nearly 30 years,
and have two children, Matthew and Suzanne. John's passions
are teaching the Bible, walking, and planning family vacations.

CPSIA information can be obtained
at www.ICGtesting.com
Printed in the USA
LVHW080920200822
726444LV00013B/1137